HIDDEN TREASURES
SECRET RICHES

DESTINY IMAGE BOOKS BY ANDREW WHITE

The Glory Zone in the War Zone

HIDDEN TREASURES
SECRET RICHES

*Experiencing
Solitude as a Place
of Divine Encounter*

ANDREW WHITE
VICAR OF BAGHDAD

DESTINY IMAGE® PUBLISHERS, INC.

P.O. Box 310, Shippensburg, PA 17257-0310

"Promoting Inspired Lives."

This book and all other Destiny Image and Destiny Image Fiction books are available at Christian bookstores and distributors worldwide.

Cover design by: Eileen Rockwell

For more information on foreign distributors, call 717-532-3040.

Reach us on the Internet: www.destinyimage.com.

ISBN 13 TP: 978-0-7684-5687-5

ISBN 13 eBook: 978-0-7684-5688-2

For Worldwide Distribution, Printed in the U.S.A.

1 2 3 4 5 6 7 8 / 24 23 22 21 20

DEDICATION

I dedicate this book to all of those around the world who join me in their desire for and pursuit of the secret place.

He knows that His treasuries abound: The keys of His treasuries He has put into our hands, He has made the Cross our treasurer to open for us the gates of Paradise.

—EPHRAIM THE SYRIAN

CONTENTS

INTRODUCTION

Throughout life, we all experience times of confinement, enclosure, and solitude. Sometimes this is a choice; at other times, an imposition. Throughout the history of mankind, towns, regions, or even whole nations have experienced siege and lockdown. God, however, is never on lockdown. He reigns sovereign and supreme from His throne and His voice is ever-speaking. Yes, on one level Jesus is being retained in the heavens until the restoration of all things (referred to in Acts 3:21); however, Heaven desires to invade earth right here and right now.

Christ in you is limitless; He is the glory inside of you. Holy Spirit is limitless. He is ever inspiring, energizing, counseling, whispering, breathing, fortifying, uplifting, encouraging, and illuminating the Father and the Son. As each part of the Godhead glorifies the other, those who surround the throne of glory are singing "Holy, Holy, Holy," for the revelation of His beauty and majesty is unending. Those worshiping around the throne are not experiencing confinement, claustrophobia, or monotony. In Heaven everything is moving, everything is flowing, nothing is static, stale, or stagnant. Heaven is full of movement, full of sound vibrating with fragrant beauty and pulsating with life.

As global affairs progress, we find ourselves constantly dealing with challenges that seek to distract us from the reality of the Kingdom of Heaven within and around us. Most issues we face are, in essence, not new; rather, they are evidence of history repeating itself; evidence of the cosmic war between good and evil being played out on the political, religious, educational, ethical, and individual stages of our world; and evidence of prophecy being fulfilled.

As darkness intensifies, so will the light, and this light will eventually dominate the entire world as the knowledge of divine glory covers the earth as the waters cover the sea. Within every challenge—global, national, regional, and individual—we must be aware of the redemptive and restorative heart of the King Jesus. We must adopt a Kingdom perspective to every aspect of life from our singular identity in Him to our identity as a beloved planet. If we have not done so already, we must catch a vision to see multitudes of souls reconciled to Christ, renewing their faith, fortifying their families, resetting priorities, embracing Jesus as their first love, and longing to experience the unsearchable riches of Christ.

Just as God was always with His people in times past, He is intimately involved in global activity on a micro level and on a macro level in our day. Across the globe, we are being surrounded by many dramatic, divine transformations that many are not noticing. In many places I see fragmentation turning into consolidation, frenzy turning into calm, apathy and passivity turning into action, and blindness turning into vision. In many places I see distraction turning into concentration, introspective self-orientation turning into kindness and communal love, and hurried impatience turning into gracious sensitivity. Again, in many places I see ingratitude, presumption, and entitlement turning into appreciation and preference of others; pride and egoism turning into humility; and rebellion turning into repentance.

In other places, I see the public place turning into the inner chamber, the spaces of entertainment turning into the "upper room." I see old wells being reopened and denominational rivalry being overridden by the rise of one singular united army and one radiant bride. I see preoccupation with trivia turning into a renewed focus on that which matters, and deformed worldviews become reformed. I am certainly not suggesting that any of these reversals of transformations are in way complete; there is immense work to be done. However, I am starting to see an "overturning of the tables" and a modification and adjustment of attitudes, mindsets, priorities, methodologies, and opinions. Where renaissance and reformation are in seed form and where transformation is latent and dormant, I say, "Let them come forth to fullness for such a time as this."

Those who truly fall in love with Jesus and set their eyes on the things above and become preoccupied with the divine activity of Heaven rather than focusing on the activity of hell will undoubtedly step into a greater alignment and preparation for the greater glory to come. New mandates, fresh mantles, directives, and great assignments are coming for those who discard the worthless and dwell in the secret place of His presence. We must evaluate our positions in order to revalue His presence. Only those who know their God will do great exploits. His presence is more precious than all the silver and gold that the world could contain. His presence is of priceless worth. I repeat, there is a call to reevaluate our position and to revalue His presence.

We must renew our intentionality of releasing love, compassion, and assistance to others. We must refuse to discard or belittle the feelings of those who feel secluded, marginalized, forgotten, and those who live in terror and fear. We must say "no" to passivity, apathy, nonchalance, and indifference. We must allow the one united, coherent, harmonious, precise, resonating, life-filled, eternal, covenantal voice of Heaven to override the multiple, divided, self-contradictory, distorted soundtracks of the media. We must return to the secret place individually and corporately in order to receive a fresh anointing and fill our horns with fresh oil. We must intentionally prepare ourselves and each other to stand unitedly and say "yes" to Heaven's agenda in our time.

Throughout this book, I want to take you on a journey, a very real journey. Together we will explore the priceless value of solitude with God, and we will discuss the hidden riches of the secret place. We will consider the great invitation of God to "step aside" as Moses did when he saw the burning bush. We will reflect on the resounding call to "come away" with Him, and the deep desire of God to make Himself accessible and manifestly present to us in times of enclosure, confinement, and even in moments of extreme involuntary isolation that are not the small spaces or desirable pauses in life that we intend to create. We will not confuse the beauty of solitude with the pain of isolation, but together we will consider how, in every space, the desire of your Father is for you to experience the unfathomable depths of His friendship and love.

First though, let me tell you about Lady Najat.

1

LADY NAJAT

Her eyes were wide and deep. She grabbed my arm and drew me close:

"Abouna, Abouna, Abouna (father, father, father), I saw Him, Abouna, it was last night...I saw Him, I saw Him, Abouna, listen I am being serious...*I saw Him, Abouna...I saw Him!*"

These were the elated cries of Lady Najat, an old refugee lady from my Iraqi community in Baghdad. Her eyes were wide, her face streaming with tears. She had hobbled up the steps from the one-roomed basement in which she lives in order to meet me at my car on the roadside. My team looked on and seemed to be as perplexed and concerned as I was. Who on earth had dear Lady Najat seen? Why was she so upset and overwhelmed with emotion? After all, there was no one really that important in Jordan other than the king.

This dear old lady proceeded to explain how, after all these years, she had finally seen Jesus. He had appeared to her during the previous night.

As my team embraced her and began to ask her more and more questions, she continued to weep and describe her encounter with Jesus in vivid detail. Somehow this dramatic encounter with Jesus did not surprise me. After all, if anyone within the tormenting oppression of feeling abandoned had already found the superior pleasures of divine friendship, it was Lady Najat.

Najat is a beautiful, dignified old lady. There is something quite regal in her posture before man and before God, which is why my team have all fallen in love with her and added the title *lady* to her name. At times she reminds me of the prophetess Anna, as she spends endless hours in her basement in worship and intercession. On one day the previous year, she had prayed literally all day for money to come to her, and as she arose from prayer I arrived at her door with a cash gift. She did not even realize that I was back in Amman, and on opening her front door she wept on my shoulder, overwhelmed by the perfect timing of a faithful God who had heard her prayer.

Lady Najat knows what confinement is. She fled terrible persecution in Baghdad, bringing with her an abandoned autistic boy whom she took under her huge, compassionate "grandmother wings." She lives in Amman in a very cold, damp basement apartment and she is too old to expend much energy. Like so many people, she fled Baghdad with no possessions, and she depends on charities and churches for support. With the current quarantine regulations and restrictions in Jordan, she cannot even attend the local market to obtain groceries. Like the rest of the refugees gratefully residing in this host country, Lady Najat is now experiencing another layer of quarantine on top of dispossession, homelessness, bereavement, displacement, and trauma.

Why am I talking to you about Lady Najat? The reason is this: Lady Najat's life is a message to be read and her daily existence embodies a striking paradox; in her own words she will tell you that she is old, yet young; she is confined, yet free; deprived, yet eternally grateful. She is saddened, yet joyful; she is powerless, yet constantly empowered.

Lady Najat is old and frail, yet her demeanor is that of a queen. She is weak, yet she is strong; she is earthbound, yet she flies like an eagle. Her tired, aged eyes have seen indescribable horror and injustice, yet those very same eyes have gazed in awe upon Him who is the very essence of beauty. Lady Najat is a "quarantined refugee" but she is also a *liberated soul* who has found a home in Jesus and who has Jesus in her home. Jesus is more than a guest in that damp, dilapidated basement; He is a resident there. He has found more than a place of visitation; He has found a place of habitation.

There is a dimension of this great paradox that I want us to journey into together in this book. I want us to explore together some of the realities and mysteries that we must embrace in this hour so that we can live and live well.

I do not want us to deny the anguish and obscurity that surrounds us, nor minimize the immense courage, sacrifice, and despair of those who are facing the fiercest of battles. I am not a person who attempts to beautify and decorate the grotesque. I do not exalt crisis nor the infringement of human rights or social justice in any of its forms. There is nothing attractive about captivity, bondage, punishment, violation, invasion, or transgression. There is nothing beautiful about feeling trapped and besieged or watching a person fight for their life.

I understand the intensity of isolation units and intensive care wards; I experienced them both as a patient and as a medic. I know what is to be taken hostage and to feel besieged; I have walked many darkened paths of bereavement, injustice, terror, imprisonment, lockdown, illness, isolation, siege, confusion, and despair. I have seen members of my congregation literally burned alive in cages. I know what terror is, and likewise I know what it is to be on the edge of life and death. From the unexpected loss of my brother in his late twenties to the persecution of my congregation in Baghdad, I have known sorrow and heartache in its most unbearable forms, yet I refuse to magnify pain. I will not hide pain by calling it something else, but I refuse to celebrate pain. I will celebrate Jesus.

From my earliest days as a five-year-old boy delivering first aid to ill people in my little wooden go-cart, my childhood soul was driven by an innate desire to eliminate physical and emotional pain from this world. I had a little tin of plasters, tissues, cotton wool, and bandages that I kept in the go-cart that my father had made for me, and my sole desire was to dress the wounds of anyone who was hurting. I would visit the old people in the neighborhood who were wounded by loneliness, and I would talk to them and drink tea with them after school in order to help relieve their pain. Desperate to see every person's anguish diminish, I did everything

I could to bring peace and relief, and my teenage desire to train as an anesthesiologist was born from this endeavor. Intellectually and emotionally energized by this single mandate to eliminate pain from people's lives, I pursued anesthesiology with passion and resolution. Yet as I found myself gradually forced to face the tragic unachievability of this great childhood ideal, I began to learn that the only true painkiller, the only true calmative, the only real analgesic was Jesus Himself.

As a medic working in war zones and spending his life visiting British, American, and Iraqi prisons; negotiating the liberation of hostages; embracing the abandoned and rejected; experiencing personal captivity; and rescuing those trapped by flames in burning homes, I am well aware of that which cannot be celebrated. I am well aware of the vanity and futility of attempting to construct and enforce some cheap, glossy theory by claiming, as some do, that every dark cloud has a silver lining. In some dark clouds there are no silver linings, and in the dark, sinister smoke clouds that rose from the homes of my congregation in war-torn Baghdad, there was no bright side.

We must mature in our thinking so that we do not confuse evil with good. God is not attempting to heal lucifer—there is no good in him. What is "good," however, is the reality that solitude is not loneliness, stillness is not paralysis, and confinement is not isolation. What is even better than "good" is that even in those dark, frozen moments of true loneliness, fear, paralysis, trauma, and isolation, His desire is to overwhelm us with His felt presence.

2

THE ONE THING

One thing I have asked from the Lord, that I shall seek: That I may dwell in the house of the Lord all the days of my life, to behold the beauty of the Lord and to meditate in His temple (Psalm 27:4).

The words of David are born from a singularity of heart and vision that in many ways crystallizes the call to fix our gaze on one alone. Many scholars state that this psalm was one of David's earlier psalms, most probably written when he was in his early twenties and on the run from King Saul.

From an early age, David had learned to value, treasure, and celebrate the audience of one. His music was born from this singularity of vision. It would be easy to dismiss such passionate resolve as being merely a natural feature of David's tempera-ment. After all, he was one of Jesse's sons; with no temple having yet been built, his home life had been his anchor. He had been raised as a God-fearing Jew from the day he was born. He was self-aware, established in his identity as "son of the covenant," and knew that God was a covenant-keeper. He was resilient and able to resist the perversion other reli-gions. He been anointed in front of his family and must have felt motivated to pursue God.

On the other hand, one could argue that as a boy David had every reason to fall into self-doubt due to the jealous dismissals of his older brothers and devote his life to the trade in which he had become so skilled. When Jesse expressed indifference to his existence and suitability for kingship, David could have easily slipped into a whole season of self-dismissal and melancholy regarding his own life, yet he did not.

It was not merely the fear of Saul that refocused David's passion and caused him to fix his gaze so unrelentingly upon the Almighty. The sense of passion, longing, and nostalgia that this psalm conveys relates to the level of divine intimacy that had so profoundly marked his life. The temple had not yet been built; the dwelling place of God was David's heart.

There must have been a level of tenacity and inner stillness that came from his expertise in shepherding, protecting and experiencing "oneness" with the land. Equally, there must have been a level of prophetic unction and a quickening in his spirit after being anointed by Samuel. However, it is clear that both the singularity of David's passion and the acute focus of his gaze were due the fact that he was a *lover*.

I believe that David was intimately in love with his Father and Creator. He had been caught up in a holy, divine romance—an intimate friendship. His heart—ever consumed with affection toward God—was being constantly tenderized toward His presence. David longed to be in that presence of God; he wanted there to be no space, no distance between himself and Him with whom his soul was consumed. He treasured his dwelling place and never wanted to be relocated or displaced from it.

We must ask ourselves: where do we live? where do we abide? where is our dwelling place? Have we truly made Him our place of habitation so that in turn He can find His place of habitation in us? As Jesus explained to dear Martha of Bethany, who did all she could to treat Him as an honored guest in her home, her sister Mary had chosen the "one thing" that mattered.

> *Only one thing is necessary, for Mary has chosen the good part, which shall not be taken away from her* (Luke 10:42).

Once again, we see this phrase—*one thing*. Mary of Bethany, like David, was a lover; she was a gazer; she had singularity of vision, and she placed the highest value on His presence. Like David who had become consumed with adoration for the invisible one, Mary's heart had tapped into the mystery, the enigma, the majesty of Him who was now the visible one. One saw the glorious Creator, and thousands of year later the other saw the glorious Son. Both had been caught up with the one thing. Both released fragrant incense. David, son of Jesse, released incense to God through meditative worship and unrelenting praise; Mary of Bethany through her physical gaze, her intentional "present-ness," and later by her physical anointing of the Son. Both had given him their undivided fascination, their attention, their meditation. Both were in awe of who He was. Both were tender and sensitive to the sweetness of His presence. Both were lovers, and both were listeners.

I believe that David and Mary of Bethany are just two examples of many who performed the highest ministry—our ministry to the Godhead. Like many others, they were two imperfect people who each placed an extremely high value on divine presence. They were both sensitive to love, and they both fixed their gaze upon the "one thing," perceiving His nearness to be an exclusive luxury.

This is our great high call. There will continue to be sacred seasons when we must set aside every distraction and every inferior pleasure (including the good, noble activities that demand our attention) in order to create a space to experience the superior pleasures of God. There are times when we must be ruthlessly intentional and unrelenting in our consecration of sacred time to be alone with Him. There are times when we must prepare a sanctuary within and around us and allow our "eagle eyes" to be "dove's eyes," eliminating all peripheral vision and fixing our gaze upon Him alone.

3

THE TREE HOUSE

When I was a young boy, I lived near the forest. In many ways the forest was our mini-paradise, our fairy-tale land on earth—a place of unlimited adventure, suspense, and freedom. The forest was an invitation to engage in all types of creative exploits that exhilarated a young boy's soul, a place where fantasy and reality seemed to converge.

My friends and I constructed our new dwelling place in a very tall oak tree on the top of a high hill, which looked down into the heart of the woods.

Our tree house was perfectly situated as it gave us an excellent viewing point and great hiding place. There were several passers-by we could spy on as it was on the main route that led to an enclosure of garden allotments where people grew all sorts of vegetables such as parsnips and carrots. The forest was a wild place, bursting with life, fragrance, texture, and movement. There were limitless sounds, resonances, and vibrations that we could feel. Our tree house was place of immense delight; we called it "The Camp." With its location being so high up and on the top of the hill, we could feel the breeze on our faces, and when the winds were strong, the sense of liberty increased.

"The Camp" was not just any normal tree house; I remember it more as a "tree-palace." Thanks to our large bundle of ropes, axes, hammers, and saws, we succeeded in building a few different levels by using planks of oak taken from other trees. As we drew near to completion, we managed with teamwork to get a big old mattress up there that my father had kept in the garden shed. We made our tree house a "resting place." We had a small array of home-made catapults, and without barely moving we were able to fire conkers (horse chestnuts) out of our hiding place in true military style. It was great that we did not have to move. We just entered our tree and fired out darts effortlessly from a place of rest and stillness.

We had worked attentively to design and build our "secret place." It took determination as we spent hours collecting wood in order to create our own ladder out of the larger, sturdy branches. We had a few other items up there, but the true luxury of our palace was a bag of broken cookies from the "broken cookie" shop. For just two pennies we could buy an enormous bag of broken cookies. There were stacks of large bags of them at the front of the store, each one carefully tied up with brown string—delivered directly from the factory—bags of broken pieces, random rejects awaiting the mouths of hungry boys. Other than our catapults, we did not keep anything else up inside the tree house—we did not need to because the place itself was our entertainment. The place itself was our joy. I did, however, keep my first-aid kit up there. Afterall, I was a "sensible," "serious" twelve-year-old and an aspiring doctor with eight years of emergency go-cart experience faithfully serving my neighbors and comrades. It would not be wise to enter "The Camp" unequipped.

On many afternoons we would fall asleep in "The Camp," lying flat on the mattress on the top deck with the sunlight shining in through the leafy branches. We went up there every Saturday after a long week at school—this secret hideout was not simply a place of excitement and adventure; it literally became our Sabbath resting place.

I remember the sense of bliss as I relaxed under the shafts of light beaming through the leaves; now and again a great glowing ray of sunlight would shine through and warm my face. I felt great peace in the tree. It was free from trouble and friction and being enclosed there made me feel empowered, protected, fearless, and elevated above the clamor and banality of the world. It was a place of intrigue, joy, and delight, a secret place of observation and contemplation that my friends and I could call our own. Often, when I was up in the tree house alone, I would talk to God. It was during a period in the Pentecostal movement when people in England would attend "waiting meetings" to wait for the Holy Spirit to "arrive." Those "waiting meetings" were so boring! I never felt the presence of God there but oh, how I did up in my tree house. In this place of beautiful confinement, I found life itself. I did not need to "wait" at any "waiting meeting," for I would feel God's presence right there surrounding me. In fact, it seemed that my heavenly Father was sitting in His own "waiting meeting"—He was right there waiting for my arrival.

There are countless lessons to be drawn from my tree house. In many ways, our "Camp" says it all: Would you let the Tree of Life be your hiding place? Would you heighten your perspective and let it be your viewing point, your place of supernatural elevation and higher revelation? Would you let the rich, green, verdant, life-breathing Tree of Life be your place of contemplation, fascination, and empowerment? Would you let its leafy branches hide you and surround you with life, peace, joy, and security? Would you let this tree be your place of sabbath rest, your hideout, your place of encounter? Would you guard your tree house and not neglect it or clutter it with unnecessary objects? Would you cherish it, build it, and cultivate it well? Would you lay down in it and absorb the piercing rays of the sun that warm your soul and illuminate your spirit as they shine through the branches? Would you be sensitive to the currents of the breeze that pass through? Would you take time to listen to the gentle rustling of its leaves as you inhale the fragrances of life itself?

Ladies and gentlemen, old ones and young ones, please listen to me: The Tree of Life is not a new-age icon; the Tree of Life is a person and His name is Jesus. Hide yourself in Him and embrace any confined space that you can find with Him. Let Him alone become your home. He is not a restrictive place; He is a limitless place. He is not a low place; He is the *Most High* place and He is a safe place. Abide in Him, dwell in Him, make your shelter in Him, find pleasure in Him, for He is altogether lovely.

I am the vine, you are the branches; he who abides in Me and I in him, he bears much fruit, for apart from Me you can do nothing (John 15:5).

The Key Is in the Tree

I have learned throughout my life that the key to every issue in life and the solution to every crisis lies in the question: Which tree am I eating from? I hear the voice even now: "There are always two trees in the garden—from which will you eat?" There is a choice presented to each of us every day. This choice is a radical, absolute choice, for in the spirit realm there is no gray area, no fusion of incompatibilities, no hybrid tree that is half the Tree of Life and half the tree of carnality and worldly rationalism.

When Adam and Eve sinned, their partaking of the forbidden fruit from the tree of the knowledge of good and evil resulted in a coronation of rationalism, intellectual pride, and earthly knowledge. Man's intellect became crowned above his spirit, and this foreign crown opened up an inferior pathway

41

toward death, disease, and destruction. They had eaten from the wrong tree. This was not a tree that was legally theirs. This was a forbidden tree, and the golden key was not in this tree. Jesus Himself now represents the Tree of life and He is the place of desire fulfilled. He is our new Eden—for Eden itself means desire, and the only place of having desires fulfilled is in Him for He Himself represents this Tree of Life. He is the place of nourishment, vision, wisdom, and sustenance and His leaves are for the healing of the nations.

The Garden Enclosed

The place of confinement and solitude may itself be considered a garden—a mini-Eden. We can create a special place where, like Adam and Eve, we find a place of deep, intimate communion and companionship with Him and allow His voice to be amplified above all others. We can turn the place of enclosure into a place of His presence filled with divine fragrance, color, fresh sounds, and everything that a physical garden offers. This is a place where our five spiritual senses are ignited and re-sensitized.

Furthermore, we can embrace the wonderous reality that the Father actually views each one of us as a fragrant garden cultivated by His dwelling there and that to Him it is also a place of refreshing delight through oneness with us.

> You are my private garden, my treasure, my bride, a secluded spring, a hidden fountain. Your thighs shelter a paradise of pomegranates with rare spices— henna with nard, nard and saffron, fragrant calamus and cinnamon, with all the trees of frankincense, myrrh, and aloes, and every other lovely spice. You are a garden fountain, a well of fresh water streaming down from Lebanon's mountains (Song of Solomon 4:12-15 NLT).

The blissful reality of intimacy with the Godhead is that the sense of mutual indwelling becomes so real and one steps into an ever-deepening knowledge of reciprocated adoration. Just as the very atmosphere of Eden, as an outpost of Heaven, was an atmosphere of intense love, the atmosphere of your home, your car, your garden, your forest walk, you beach cove becomes saturated with love. Suddenly, no fear can dwell there. You have found your private Eden and He has found Eden in you— the place of true *delight*.

4

PRESERVING THE
VALUABLE

Protecting the Seed

If anyone had experienced confinement and apprehension regarding the unknown, it must have been Noah. He had no board of counsel, no neighboring town, no news channel, no vestige of any infrastructure to rely on. Yet in accordance with the meaning of his name, Noah found a place of "rest" in faith-filled expectation. To consider that on one level the entire future of our planet, all of the genetic information and blueprints of life and the eternal plans of God in relation to the creative order established at Eden were confined within an intricately designed floating wooden structure is really quite astonishing. Due to the level of pure wonder, mystery, and enigma that these unique accounts depict, many of us grow up with them as if they are fairy tales or magical legends.

In the place of confinement, restriction, aloneness and complete strangeness, Noah, his family, and indeed the rest of the future human race that would germinate from his seed had everything they required. God had not overlooked a single detail. All forms of life, including the animal life, were being carefully preserved due to the intelligent mind of the divine Creator. The covenant-keeper was right there inside the Ark with the very race with whom He was in covenant. They were together; they were one.

With the corrupt systems of the past demolished and literally *washed away*, the post-flood era was to represent a whole new start, a literal "resetting" of the globe, and a renewal of covenant. The launch of this era would be initiated between the great preserver and covenant-keeper who placed His majestic bow within the sky and the covenant-recipient whose first act was to create an altar of worship.

Like Noah, we must cultivate a deep relationship with the invisible God through the presence of His Spirit. We must learn to trust in His covenantal, redemptive nature. We must rest on the waters of his presence and talk to the Dove.

Guarding the Presence

Consider the story of another Ark—the sacred Ark of the Covenant—that small place in which God contained His merciful, life-giving presence. We read in Chronicles of how David was fearful to return the Ark to Jerusalem due to an incident that involved God's judgement on Uzzah for carelessness, presumption, and irreverence. David thus diverted and identified a faithful guardian and safe resting place for the Ark in the home of Obed-edom.

Thus the ark of God remained with the family of Obed-edom in his house three months; and the Lord blessed the family of Obed-edom with all that he had (1 Chronicles 13:14).

The faithful stewardship of Obed-edom in his safeguarding of that which was precious resulted in great blessing on the entire household of this man. Like Noah, he was careful, reverent, attentive, prudent, and intentional in his adherence to the blueprints and instructions of Heaven.

Obed-edom knew what an honor it was to have this holy treasure hidden in his home, and it was no doubt with holy awe and gratitude that he made his home a resting place. There is much that we can learn from this episode regarding the valuing of His presence in our homes and by our families—these lessons ring loud and clear into the modern age.

When the right time arrived, the Ark was taken to its rightful place and pitched within the sacred space that David had prepared for it.

And they brought in the ark of God and placed it inside the tent which David had pitched for it (1 Chronicles 16:1).

Although the Ark had now physically left the home of Obed-edom, they eye of the Lord was still on him. The Ark had moved on, but the demonstration of divine favor and commissioning on his life and family had not, for once again he was entrusted with the protection of that which was sacred.

So he left Asaph and his relatives there before the ark of the covenant of the Lord to minister before the ark continually, as every day's work required; and Obed-edom with his 68 relatives; Obed-edom, also the son of Jeduthun, and Hosah as gatekeepers (1 Chronicles 16:37-38).

Like Obed-edom, our homes must be dwelling places of His presence. When I reflect on the periods of intense persecution, lockdowns, electricity cuts, and danger in Baghdad (for the two decades

I was there we had electricity for only four hours a day) and how families sat in circles to worship under candlelight or with torches, it reminds me of the accounts of the Early Church.

Though their faith was considered illegal by Rome, the early believers did not allow fear or constriction to prevent them from keeping the "house-fires" burning. In essence, home gatherings started prior to this period, for so often when Jesus entered a home people assembled. In this sense, Jesus enabled the essence of *church* to be modeled before it was born—*Kingdom* citizens gathered in awe around their glorious King. As He allowed people to crowd around Him in courtyards, chambers, and rooms, He was modeling a dimension of the future home church.

The New Testament refers to family homes where early believers gathered to embrace the life and message of Jesus, grow in faith, and prayerfully support each other. The book of Acts and the letters of Paul refer to the home gatherings of various men and women: Mary the mother of John Mark

(Acts 12:12), Lydia (Acts 16:40), Prisca and Aquila (Rom. 16:3,5), Nympha (Col. 4:15), Philemon and Apphia (Philem. 1-2). Whether they had been eyewitnesses or not, these gatherings kept Jesus in the forefront of their memories and minds:

> *Day by day continuing with one mind in the temple, and breaking bread from house to house, they were taking their meals together with gladness and sincerity of heart* (Acts 2:46).

Considering how brief and seemingly incidental these references to house churches appear to be, it is likely that there were several others not mentioned. These homes provided safe soil in which the roots of faith could grow strong and deep; they were places where the presence of Jesus was hosted with honor and reverence.

5

THE WARDROBE

I am sure that most of you reading this book are familiar with the classic work of C.S. Lewis, *The Lion, the Witch and the Wardrobe.* I had the honor of staying in the exact room that he had when I was a doctoral research student at Magdalen College, Cambridge. It was a longstanding college tradition for students to sign their names in the wardrobes, and each day as I opened my wardrobe I would see the signature of C.S. Lewis.

I am an admirer of C.S. Lewis' work, and often when I am teaching at Wheaton College I take my colleagues to see the original family wardrobe and the writing desk that are housed there at the Marion E. Wade Center of Wheaton College. As most will know, the basic plot of *The Lion, the Witch and the Wardrobe* follows four English children who are relocated to the large old country house of an old professor following a wartime evacuation. The youngest child, Lucy, visits a mystery land called Narnia via an old magical wardrobe that they discover in a spare room. Lucy's three siblings are with her on her third visit, and as the adventure unfolds they find themselves in an epic drama to save Narnia and preserve their own lives.

As I was writing this chapter, I heard the Holy Spirit say these simple words. "Without the wardrobe, there is no Narnia." The simple message is this: If you remove the secret place from your life and despise the place of solitude with God, you are depriving yourself of a great dramatic, supernatural adventure with Him and preventing the full narrative of your life being written. Had the children in the novel not been intentional about entering that which appeared to be the dull, boring, unfamiliar place, they would have deprived themselves of joyful entry into the limitless realm of adventure that awaited them the other side of the wardrobe.

Divine Adventures

The famous wardrobe, as described in the novel, is nothing extraordinary—just a regular everyday wardrobe with a back that appears solid. There is no hint or suggestion in its design that it could lead to some mystical place beyond the banality of the world. The historical setting of the story is the crisis of a global war (World War II) and the 1940 forced evacuation, which caused the children to be relocated to this rural house that was home to the magical wardrobe.

Global and national crisis and calamity were causing fear, death, restriction, closure, upheaval, and displacement. The children were now in a new place—a strange, unfamiliar place. In this new place they entered a wardrobe—place of further confinement—in order to access a whole new reality, a whole new dynamic, and a whole new approach to life. They became caught up in a heavenly drama, and here in this place secret knowledge and revelation were imparted to them. They received new senses and an entirely new level of perceptivity and awareness. They started to need and appreciate each other like never before, and they became one and congruent with the realm into which they had stepped.

Maybe the scenario feels strangely familiar. The difference being that the individual and corporate call to the secret place is not an invitation to some fantasy, fairy-tale world nor a mere form of psychological escapism and self-indulgence that calls us to deny and despise the natural world and "neutralize" fear. Rather, this great high call relates to posturing ourselves as Samuel did before the ark, lingering in His presence as Joshua, and embracing the new covenant assurance that we are already seated in heavenly places. In this sense we are already in Narnia—we are already in the realm of victory where the lion has defeated the witch. We must rest in this knowledge and reembrace the glory of the

Lion of Judah so we can reacquaint ourselves with our true identity and our true position.

Maybe for some of us it is time to enter or reenter the wardrobe, time to be still and enter the secret place, time to journey into the realm of divine supernatural glory. Maybe it is time to experience the joyful ecstasy and bliss of being in His presence. Maybe it is time for visitations, visions, dreams, apparitions and fresh dialogues with God—time to push through the place of restriction, fear, banality, and the mundane and optimize our experience of it by seeing it as a gateway, a threshold into another realm just as the wardrobe was.

Divine Enlightenment

One of the paradoxes of life is that the greatest treasures are often found in the darkest places. Whether the seed in the soil, the child in the womb, or the photograph in the dark room, the dark place becomes a place of growth and development. Those who are in Jesus can know constant light, for in the darkest places he is light—*Light* in us, the hope of glory. The Father is the Father of Lights and His spirit is the great illuminator and enlightener who leads us into all truth. In His Light, we see light. The paradox of the dark place, the place of enclosure and hiding (whether physically or atmospherically and spiritually dark) is that when we fix our eyes upon Jesus, we experience His light filling our soul and igniting us with fresh truth, awe, and revelation. We start to partake of the treasures of the darkness, and we remember that without the night sky we cannot gaze at the stars.

6

GLORY IN THE CAVES

Whether on childhood visits to the caves of Chislehurst in the south of England, in which children hid during the war, or further out toward the Greek islands, I have always been greatly intrigued by caves. It is easy to appreciate the heights of mountaintops as the places of exalted and expansive views, unfolding revelation, blissful altitude, and spiritual exhilaration. Yet the true majesty of the mountain resides not simply in its magnificent peaks and spectacular pinnacles but equally in its hidden homes that lie amidst the rocks.

The Middle Eastern landscape of desert land, mountains, valleys, creeks, rocks, caves, springs, and streams was a rich part of my experience during the decades of my work out there. I often explored the caves and strongholds of David in En Gedi and, particularly, the caves in Jericho. There is something deeply fascinating about rock formation and texture, and while I enjoy experiencing mountaintops and absorbing the dramatic geological and topographical diversity of Israel with its plains, valleys, gardens, vineyards, rivers, lakes, and desert regions, there is something equally exhilarating about "entering" the mountain and stepping into the caves, crevices, and gorges in and beneath the rocks. I enjoy observing sudden shafts of light penetrate the darkness, and I love the silence and the profound sense of mystery, history, and seclusion of the caves, for one can feel therein the weight of history and stories untold.

One of my most profound cave experiences was in Jericho. It was during the late eighties after my initial period of study in Jerusalem, and I was in a very remote location on my way to visit a secluded monastery, which could be accessed only via a very steep slope up the mountain side. There was no path or road, only mountain rocks and caverns. Gaining access to this monastery was one of the most complicated and tedious journeys I have ever experienced, yet one I shall never forget.

Unusually for me, I was completely alone and my journey toward the monastery felt like a true pilgrimage. When I eventually finally arrived there, I was perplexed at how anybody could live and meditate in this remote place. I can remember continually asking myself how they even brought food to this remote place. I met the three Greek orthodox monks who lived up there and they welcomed me with open arms. It turned out that in the vicinity there was a very small water spring, which created a continuous natural waterfall. Several historians suggest this area of the region was likely to be the very place that Jesus came for His forty-day fast prior to beginning His ministry. I spent the whole day in this remote place and felt deeply overwhelmed by the sense of mystery, majesty, serenity, and tranquility that flooded my soul while I was there.

After leaving the confined compound, I visited several of the monastic caves used by the monks as sacred places for times of intense contemplation. I identified one cave in particular which my spirit was very drawn to. I desired to experience the tangible, manifest presence of God in the way so many of the monastic and mystical communities had throughout the ages. I wanted to feel His closeness and His love in a new way.

> As I see it, contemplative prayer is simply an intimate sharing between friends. It's about frequently taking time to be alone with the One we know loves us.[1]

The Rock in the Cave

As I entered the enclosure, I saw a large rock, which was used as a seat; people had carved images of crosses into the cave wall, and I too did the same. Herein I found a perfect sanctuary that was shading me from the blazing heat. As I peered out of the cave entrance, I was overwhelmed by the fine view of the Dead Sea in the distance. Then, as I quietened my excited mind, I said to God, "I know that

Your Spirit is with me and I am so grateful for all that You have done in my life." Then I began to meditate on the temptations that Jesus faced, and I became deeply aware of how possible it would have been for Him to yield to any of these temptations. We often read about the temptations, and in our familiarity we unknowingly reduce their status to those of "difficult challenges." Yet we must remember that the Son of God set aside His deity and faced the evil one as the Son of Man. As I sat in the cave and pondered on the magnitude of what had taken place on our behalf, I began to weep. As my tears continued, I received a fresh revelation of how victorious, loyal, and sinless Jesus was.

It was here in the seclusion of my new sanctuary that I had one of a few physical angelic encounters that I was to experience in Israel. I had experienced angels in Bethlehem in the West Bank (and later the visible presence of angels would be part of our daily life in Baghdad—this I describe in my book, *The Glory Zone in the War Zone*), but I had never had physical angelic encounters or experiences with angels elsewhere in Israel. The angel appeared in the cave, and like many of the others I later would meet he was large, winged, clothed in white; his face was radiant, smiling, and full of joy. The angel did not speak but stood silently in front of me in the cave, so I asked him a question: "What is God saying to me here?" I was expecting him to reply but he simply continued to smile at me in silence, and as he did I felt tangible waves of peace wash over me.

After an hour or so, I took a walk to absorb the views then returned to the cave as I knew I needed to embrace the moment. I needed to stop "doing" and learn to "be." I needed to embrace the sacredness of "now." Over the years, I continued to visit that monastery and its surrounding caves, and, on occasion, others accompanied me. I still deeply cherish the memories of my first visit. It was here as a young student in Israel that I had stepped into one of the most intense and awe-filled moments of my life, an experience that had altered my perspective and changed my expectation of life forever. Though I knew my path ahead would not involve a monastic life, I was deeply aware that solitude with

God would be a secret treasure that paved this path with gold.

The Cave as a Birthplace

For Mary and Joseph, the cave was literally a birthing place. The "rock of ages" was birthed in a cave. He who became the chief cornerstone was birthed in the Shepherd's shelter. Not only were caves places for birth but they were also locations for resuscitation, resurrection, and intense divine activity. For Lazarus, for Jesus, and for those who rose from their graves when Jesus was crucified (see Matt. 27:52-53), the cave was a place of glorious revival and resurrection.

It is often this way for us—we must cultivate our place of solitude with God and allow this secret place to be the place of incubation, the place of birthing, and the place of revival. Allow the triune God to draw you into Himself, the Most Holy Place; ask Him to impart fresh revelation, implant seeds of fresh vision into your spirit, and endow you with fresh counsel, wisdom, directives, ideas, and assignments for the days ahead. Do not run from the cave; carve His name and your name in the wall; explore its interior and enjoy this new place of divine dialogue.

We must place ourselves in the rock as Moses did and understand that this rock is no less than God Himself. We must allow the Godhead to be our hiding place, for in this place of friendship and communion we will experience increasing measures of His glory.

> *Behold, there is a place by Me, and you shall stand there on the rock; and it will come about, while My glory is passing by, that I will put you in the cleft of the rock and cover you with My hand until I have passed by* (Exodus 33:21-22).

The secluded place can be a place of tender nurturing and cultivation—do not buy into the lie that in quietness and aloneness you are emotionally or spiritually restricted, for here, in stillness with Him, you can be totally free. You will experience His hand of covering and protection just as the newborn Moses did as he floated in that confined basket along the waters of his destiny. Consider too how John the Baptist danced inside the womb as he travelled inside of Elizabeth to see the Messiah. The place of darkness and restriction was already his place of incubation—this place of incubation became a place of profound recognition, conversation, interaction, spiritual impartation, and exuberant joy.

The Cave of Adullam: Refuge and Retreat

On one occasion when David was fleeing from Saul, who was trying to kill him, he sought refuge among the Philistines in Gath (see 1 Sam. 21:10-14). Realizing, however, that his life was in peril, he left Gath and escaped to the Cave of Adullam. The origin of this name *Adullam* signifies "refuge" or "retreat."

> *So David departed from there and escaped to the cave of Adullam; and when his broth-ers and all his father's household heard of it, they went down there to him. Everyone who was in distress, and everyone who was in debt, and everyone who was discontented*

gathered to him; and he became captain over them. Now there were about four hundred men with him (1 Samuel 22:1-2).

This secluded cave literally became an apostolic base of operations for David and the home of a great ministry of compassion. The fugitive in the cave became the leader of a band of "outlaws" who grew in military valor and performed great exploits. If, as historians indicate, Adullam was near the border of the Philistine lands, the location itself would have provided a level of protection for David as Saul would not have been able to launch a military operation without risking attack from the Philistines.

It says in 1 Samuel 22:1-3 that David was at the cave, and the following verse refers to it as a "stronghold" there. It is likely that David had fortified the cave, building upon its natural potential for safety. The hiding place became a military outpost, a place of prayer, divine strategic counsel, and fortification. As David knew from past seasons, God would not abandon him in the day of trouble.

For in the day of trouble He will conceal me
in His tabernacle; in the secret place of His
tent He will hide me; He will lift me up on a
rock (Psalm 27:5).

Three of David's mighty men met him there at the rock of the Cave of Adullam when the Philistines were encamped around the cave threatening him. In this time of challenge, David expressed a desire for water from the well near the gate of Bethlehem, his hometown. Three of his courageous men broke through the Philistine lines, drew water from the well, and brought it back to him.

There are lessons to be drawn from this entire event. We must never underestimate the level of divine equipping and impartation that takes place in the hidden place. Never despise the cave.

It was in the caves that David wrote at least three of his most moving psalms—Psalm 34, in which David blesses his praiseworthy, faithful, protector; Psalm 57, which affirms divine justice, recompense, and deliverance including God's dealings with enemies who set traps for us; and Psalm 142, which describes how intimately He knows us and desires to do us good.

The secret caves are the places of heavenly counsel and commissioning; they are often the places were divine directives are given, oracles released, and the champions of tomorrow established in their call. Just as Elijah was forced into hiding in the cave at Horeb after fleeing the wicked, spiteful Jezebel (see 1 Kings 19), there are people who may feel literally "forced" into a place of hiding with God because of surrounding attacks. If that is you, take courage from the story of Elijah, for whom the cave revealed itself to be a place of divine conversation, counsel, and protection.

Out of the caves, I see an emergence of courageous, tenacious, well-grounded men and women. Out of the caves I see humble heroes who have learned to lie low and who actually understand what ministry looks like. Out of the hidden place, fresh mantles and assignments will be given. Out of those difficult moments when you feel surrounded by enmity and threat, you will receive fresh stamina, courage, and resoluteness to advance the kingdom. In those dark hiding places, receive an infusion of renewed energy to run once again and, like David's men, draw from the wells of salvation that the thirsty may be refreshed.

Consider the life and preparation of John the Baptist. He was a man well acquainted with solitude and simplicity. Seclusion was itself the very essence of his unlimited spiritual freedom and development. In all of his dwelling places, John experienced an intimate revelatory dialogue with Him whom he had already encountered before birth. John experienced the divine presence of the Godhead in the womb, at home in the hill country, in desert caves, in the Jordan River, and later in the dungeon. Lying in those desert caverns in the coldness of night, a blazing furnace burned ardently within his heart. His soul ignited with passion and purpose; all of his being aligned with Heaven as he prepared to introduce Israel to her Messiah. It was a furnace that many of the third and fourth century Palestinian,

Arabian, and Persian hermits known as the "Desert Fathers" would later experience.

The solitary cave is thus the place of divine encounter, angelic visitation, incubation, birth, resuscitation, and resurrection. It is the equipping center for apostolic builders and "sent" ones. It is the place of hidden scrolls and oracles for the prophet, the place of divine counsel and revelation for the teachers and pastors, and the place from which the preparers, pioneers, revivalists, and evangelists are unleashed.

> *I will give you the treasures of darkness and hidden wealth of secret places, so that you may know that it is I, the Lord, the God of Israel, who calls you by your name* (Isaiah 45:3).

Consider the gold mines, the diamond mines, and the oil wells. Consider the deep, dark, deathly coal pits of Wales that became home to one of the most blazing revivals that the world has ever seen. Do not discard the dark places; do not miss the hidden treasures within the darkness.

Note

1. Teresa of Avila, Mirabai Starr, ed., *Teresa of Avila: The Book of My Life* (Boston, MA: New Seeds Books, 2008), 53.

7

PROTECTING THE PROPHETIC

When I consider the secluded place as being the place of protecting secret treasures and hidden riches, I reflect on the 1947 discovery of the dead sea scrolls written in Hebrew and Aramaic, dating as far back as the last three centuries BCE. The dead sea scrolls were found in seven hidden caves known as the Qumran caves in the Judean desert near the Dead Sea in the West Bank (then part of Jordan) and contained many of the most ancient forms of the Torah, and they form almost all of our Old Testament.

It is said that the scrolls were found by young Bedouin shepherds who were searching for a stray lamb in a series of small caves. When one of the boys threw a rock inside, they heard the sound of a shattering vessel and on entering the cave they discovered a large collection of jars or vases being used as storage pots for ancient scrolls made out of animal hide.

The Shrine of the Book museum in Jerusalem was built as a repository for the first seven scrolls discovered in 1947. It has a unique white dome which represents the lids of the jars in which the first scrolls were found. Some of the scrolls were actually held by the family of a great friend of mine—the Kando family—who, to this day, still own one of the original pots and keep it in their famous antique shop near to the entrance to Bethlehem. I always visit them when I am there.

When I reflect on the centuries of divine preservation and the discovery of these priceless jewels by young shepherd boys, I consider the shepherds in Bethlehem who were similarly commissioned to locate the "Word" hidden in a dark cave. God uses the humble, not the proud, in order to reveal Himself to humanity.

Within the dark confines of a small cave, God had preserved and protected His word. And who at that time would have thought that, centuries later, light would once again emerge out of darkness? The Dark Ages became the age of the printing press, and Johannes Guttenberg's famous press was the most important invention of this period. This groundbreaking, revolutionary innovation wrenched control of information and distribution from the State and the Church and laid the path for the Protestant Reformation as well as enabling the education of the masses.

When one considers a few aspects of the young Guttenberg's life prior to this world-changing innovation—and the eventual publication of the Guttenberg Bible—the symbolism is quite inspiring.

Having relocated from Mainz in Germany to Strasbourg in France, Johannes Guttenberg began his career as a goldsmith. He was from a line of highly respected specialists who held hereditary positions in goldsmithing and metal work including minting and coining. Certain of his ancestors had a seat in assessing coin forgery cases and records also indicate that he would instruct wealthy tradesmen on how to polish gems.

Later in his life, following a financial misadventure due to a very severe flood in the region, which delayed an exhibition of polished mirrors, Guttenberg (in order to satisfy his investors) referred to a great secret he had that was soon to be unveiled. This undisclosed information was a secret treasure and one of several hidden riches that would change the world and that enable the Word of God to spread like fire across the globe.

Guttenberg was a man who from a young age had learned to recognize and treasure the valuable; he was well acquainted with notions of pricelessness, sacredness, and infinite worth. He was a goldsmith who God had singled out to enlighten with new knowledge and release "a secret treasure" to the entire world. Had the terrible flood and ensuing bankruptcy not happened, Guttenberg may have never stepped out of one trade into another. He may never have experienced the dissatisfaction that propelled him to open his mind to fresh enlightenment and inspiration. God had already planned that from the place of dark despair and financial debt, a global illumination was to be released to and through this man. What was meant to harm a small French region, God turned to the good of the entire globe. From the spirits of the ancient prophets, eyewitnesses, and faithful scribes—to the scrolls in Qumran—to the candle-lit room in Guttenberg's house, God was watching over the treasures of His Word.

Gloriously "Contained"

When I think of confinement, I think of Jonah whose influence in Nineveh continued well beyond his visit in the eighth century BCE. It is clear that centuries later when St. Thomas came to Nineveh there was a strong believing community within the Abrahamic tradition and that Jonah's ministry of repentance and mercy had continued to reap a harvest of God-fearing citizens. When Thomas arrived after the time of Christ, he informed the people of Nineveh about the life, death, and resurrection of Jesus of Nazareth, the promised Messiah, and of the need to follow Him for His blood was now on the mercy seat. As a result of this, the very first Christian community in the whole of Mesopotamia (modern-day Iraq) was created in Nineveh. This legacy has continued until this day, and the remnant Christian believers in Iraq are still referred to as Assyrians—the very people who became my congregation in Baghdad. Despite most of our church community being Baghdadi, they would all consider Nineveh their traditional home and most would return there during breaks. Many had family and homes there and considered Nineveh their familial and spiritual "homeland." This is why so many Christians quickly returned there when radical terrorist groups moved into Baghdad.

God's enforcement of His will though the events of Jonah's life may have seemed punitive and unjust, but His mercy was first being displayed to Jonah through the very act of confinement. God could have easily killed Jonah and replaced him with another prophet. However, instead, by graciously ensuring the preservation of the prophetic oracle confined within Jonah—who himself was confined within the dark interior of a large fish—God was actually performing an act of double divine protection.

I often wonder what Jonah experienced spiritually as he journeyed through the waters. Did he have dreams and visions? Imagine the divine activity that must have taken place in the unseen realm as he was literally "locked" inside that fish. What we do know is that this place of confinement became both a form of protection and a form of transport and advancement toward an ordained destination.

Jonah was forced into a dramatic lockdown and God saw to it that the oracle he was carrying was not miscarried, aborted, or displaced. Despite the fight within Jonah's heart, He would be faithful to His Word and merciful in His preservation of both the prophet and the people.

Let us also consider Elizabeth, the mother of John the Baptist. Luke reports that: *"After these days Elizabeth his wife became pregnant, and she kept herself in seclusion"* (Luke 1:24). This seclusion in the remoteness of the hill country was not simply a form of self-protection from gossipers, slanderers, negative attention and conjecture, jealous glances, unnecessary exposure, and false accusation. Nor was it simply protection against interrogation regarding the validity of this "double miracle."

This place of confinement was also a place of great meditation, contemplation, and dialogue with God. I sense when reading scripture that Elizabeth had already had a dialogue with Heaven about Mary in the same way that Gabriel had visited Mary. We do not know the facts but if we view the divine activity both within and surrounding the narrative, we can be certain that Elizabeth was receiving revelation and counsel from Heaven during her time of confinement. As with Mary, Elizabeth was an expectant mother who was herself being birthed into her assignment. Along with their babies, these mothers were both also in a place of incubation and rapid growth—their assignments soon to be unveiled and established as they prepared to step into the great historical call on their lives. Divine oracles were abounding within and around them. Do not for one moment think that God cannot speak to you in the place of confinement. Often this is the very purpose of the confinement. There must be a seeding of the word in order for it to grow and flourish. Our internal climate needs to be rest so that we can nurture and cultivate that which is destined to grow in each given season.

Consider Zacharias. He was rendered mute, yet out of the restricted voice—the "non-voice"—a new voice had been spoken into being. Out of silence and "voiceless-ness," he too would have had deep dialogues with God and with angels. He too would have known the constant confirming of the word of truth until the ordained moment for the opening of his mouth arrived. He too was in a place of stillness, restriction, and incubation—the divine oracle was being nurtured and cultivated inside his spirit, and it could not be unleashed until the birth of his miracle son. Once the physical womb of the mother opened and released the prophet (the new voice) from restriction and hiding—into a new limitless space of being—the prophetic voice of his father opened from its place of restriction and was released into the atmosphere. The witnesses were in place and in the child was established and confirmed in his call. Is this not an awe-inspiring example of the perfect mind of God?

I believe that some of you reading this are literally right now having your voices "tuned" for a new sound that is soon to be released from you into a new open space. Some of you are feeling muted, confined, and restrained by silence, but actually there are world-changing oracles, songs, ideas being incubated inside of you. Some of you are literally conceiving new voices that are not yet ready to be released. Trust in God's perfect timing. For some of you, there is a resounding voice of worship, a new melody, a prophetic oracle, a voice of social justice, a media voice, a governmental voice, or an educational voice being conceived, nurtured, and prepared right there in the secret place. Let us not allow our ignorance, confusion, disillusionment, or short-sightedness to minimize or diminish the incredibly powerful things that God may be doing in this season. Let us be like Elizabeth, Mary, and Zacharias who from stillness, silent pondering, seclusion, and silence submitted themselves to divine preparation and aligned themselves with Heaven's purposes.

I will never forget the time during my student days in Jerusalem when the powerfully anointed prophetess Ruth Ward Heflin approached me at the end of a glory gathering and prophesied over me regarding the very specific call on of God on my life. This word propelled me into whole new dimension of faith and expectation.

Rather than pressing "play" and returning to regular academic and biblical study in Jerusalem, I felt compelled to run away to a quiet place and ponder on the great oracle that had just been released to me. I heard the call of the divine beloved drawing me to "come away" with Him, so I journeyed up to Galilee to pray in solitude and allow the Word to resonate and establish itself deep within my spirit.

The one I love calls to me:

The Bridegroom-King Arise, my dearest. Hurry, my darling. Come away with me! (Song of Solomon 2:10-12 TPT)

There alone, in a secluded spot on the shores of the lake, I had one of the most profound Holy Spirit encounters of my life. I was deeply aware of the all-consuming presence of God and wanted to stay there forever. It may bring a smile to your face to know that this was also the one time in my life that I fell into a deep sleep in the blazing sun and got seriously sunburned. I was burning inside and out!

When we protect the prophetic and create a space for Heaven's activities to flow in and through us, we gain a great reward. Consider the Shunammite woman who nurtured the prophet Elisha:

> Please, let us make a little walled upper chamber and let us set a bed for him there, and a table and a chair and a lampstand; and it shall be, when he comes to us, that he can turn in there (2 Kings 4:10).

This was a woman of honor! She approached her husband and gained his permission and agreement to create a space for the prophet to rest and feel at home. What a wonderful gesture this was. As I travel from nation to nation, I have been so blessed by countless women, men, and children of honor of all nationalities who have provided me with outstanding hospitality and a place to rest both physically and spiritually, and these acts of hospitality are a precious ministry.

By acting as she did, this Shunammite lady was not simply protecting the prophet and his oracle, for unbeknownst to her she was positioning herself to receive the prophet's reward. As the story unfolds, we see that God would use Elisha to birth a whole new dimension of life into this lady both physically and spiritually. Just as she had recognized and esteemed the anointing on the prophet, God was about to intervene in her circumstances and return honor and recognition to her and her husband.

8

THE EVER-SPEAKING, EVER-SINGING VOICE

One of my greatest joys is to hear the birds sing. I live in a rural area of England and the diversity of trees and birds in my locality is overwhelming. Each morning I awake to an incredible soul-lifting symphony of worship. Even when my colleagues call me from their gardens or when they are walking in the hills, I hear the birds' voices around them before I hear theirs and I often comment on the stunning background melody that I can here. I feel elated just by imagining the sounds that filled the garden of Eden.

I remember when recently burying my mother, we stood in silence around her graveside with the cold weather of early February suddenly being disrupted by a day of warmth and sun. There was a sudden change of season on that burial day, and as we stood in silence beneath the sun, the birds began to break the silence and sing joyfully from the tree that overlooked her grave. My dear mother was also a person who loved to hear the sounds of the birds. We always have plenty of seed for them to eat and they love to congregate in our gardens.

I was deprived of such joys in Baghdad; the soundtrack there was (at least in the physical realm) unequally divided between the joyful, corporate worship of our community and the sound of helicopters, earth-quaking bombs, explosions, car horns, people shouting and screaming in terror, ear-piercing emergency and warning sirens. The sky was polluted, and Baghdad was not a thriving place for birds. In fact, during my years in the war zone, I was acutely aware of the absence of birds singing, and returning home to my family in rural England consisted of returning to a different soundtrack.

Many of us need to re-sensitize both our physical and spiritual ears to receive a new soundtrack. Certain of us have literally lost our ability to listen. This may be due to the bombardment of negativity from the media, the overload of soundtracks. When so many compete for our attention, it causes our listening to become fragmented, passive, and surficial. In moments of "option overload," we hear a little of everything but truly listen to nothing. Busy agendas can push us into so much hearing that we simply do not have time to listen. It may be that there is so much disruption, distraction, and conversation in our world we no longer distinguish between noise and sound. Like our eyes, our ears are one of our five major senses and one of our five spiritual gateways. Do we need to give our senses back to our Creator and ask Him to sanctify them?

We are currently living in the most distracted generation that this planet has hosted. There is a great battle of soundtracks as multiple spiritual, political, and ideological agendas compete to dominate the airwaves. The art of listening has consequently becoming a lost art, and it is one of the primary arts that the church much fight to restore.

The restoration of listening starts with each individual choosing to rise above the noise pollution and the agitation that congests the air and find a space of noiselessness. It starts with valuing and guarding those moments of "Selah" when we press "pause" and find space to ponder, meditate, and actively listen.

> We too are called to withdraw at certain intervals into deeper silence and aloneness with God, together as a community as well as personally; to be alone with Him—not with our books, thoughts, and memories but completely stripped of everything—to dwell lovingly in His presence, silent, empty, expectant, and motionless. We cannot find God in noise or agitation.[1]

I have learned that the best learners are the best listeners. It is important to maintain a teachable spirit before God and listen to Him. His speech may come directly through a sense of knowing, an inner or outer audible voice, a vision, or an angelic encounter. His speech may flow to you from His Word or through the godly counsel of others who are themselves listening to Him. How God speaks is not our choice, but it most certainly is our responsibility to listen.

It is essential in this hour that we deeply acquaint ourselves with the Shepherd's voice. Those who are not His sheep do not know His voice; those who are His sheep know His voice. Why is it, therefore, that so many of us are not taking the time to acquaint ourselves with His voice? Could it be that we have spent so much time "doing" and that we have devalued "being"? To be with Him is to listen to Him. Let us repent from those times when we have not been ready listeners, and let us adopt the posture of Habakkuk:

I will stand on my guard post and station myself on the rampart; and I will keep watch to see what He will speak to me, and how I may reply when I am reproved. Then the Lord answered me and said, "Record the vision and inscribe it on tablets, that the one who reads it may run. For the vision is yet for the appointed time; it hastens toward the goal and it will not fail. Though it tarries, wait for it; for it will certainly come, it will not delay" (Habakkuk 2:1-3).

Interestingly, the name *Habakkuk* means "ardent embrace" and, in this context, it speaks of the prophet's whole-hearted, resolute passion to receive, record, and rely on accurate divine information. This is the mark of a faithful, steadfast, single-minded servant of the Lord. Habakkuk was intent and unwavering and decisive in his call to posture himself in stillness and alertness and be a trustworthy mouthpiece of God to his people.

Simeon was also a man who lived out the meaning of his name. *Simeon* means "one who listens," and this is exactly what Simeon did. He was probably a seer and a dreamer as well as an acute listener. He was a faithful, absorbent, receptive "high capacity" holding place for the Word of the Lord regarding the length of his own days, the identity and call of the Messiah's parents, the birth and mission of the Messiah, the deliverance of Israel, and the ingathering of the nations. This tells me that he was highly accurate and acute in his hearing. Simeon was able to hear the Word of the Lord for every circle starting from the "inner circle" of his own personal life at the epicenter, rippling out to the divine cosmic activity and the colossal inclusion of the entire human race into the covenantal relationship with the Almighty. Simeon had heard John's words of John 3:16—that God so loved us and gave His Son that none would perish—before John was ever born. Oh readers, let us never lose our awe. Is He not faithful to speak to those who will listen?

Throughout scripture there are men and women of every age who, like Simeon, visibly lived out the meaning of their names and who saw and heard God with constancy and precision. The key to spiritual receptivity is to have an undistracted mind; the key to knowing the Shepherd's voice is to spend time in the presence of the Shepherd. The key to hearing the sound of Heaven and having one's inner ears awakened to new sounds, tones, rhythms, lyrics, messages, melodies, and soundtracks relies on the disintegration of every inferior soundtrack. To listen to the birds, you must be in the correct location.

The words of that old children's song come to mind. Though the author of the song is unknown and anonymous, the message is essentially from God Himself:

> "O be careful little ears what you hear
>
> O be careful little ears what you hear
>
> for the Father up above
>
> is looking down in love."

Be a wise, intentional, prudent, and reverential listener. Allow His voice—the sound of many waters—to stream into your innermost being and bring refreshing to your soul. As you allow His voice to become known to you, the love bond between

Shepherd and sheep will deepen and you will have a renewed sense of what it means to be His prized possession.

Note

1. Mother Teresa, *In the Heart of the World: Thoughts, Stories and Prayers by Mother Teresa* (Novato, CA: New World Library, 2010), 21.

9

THE STORY OF
ABU YOUSEF

I want to tell you the story of Abu Yousef. Abu Yousef was an old, frail Iraqi man in his eighties and one of the few people in my community who was completely blind. Abu Yousef has now graduated to glory, but during my time in Baghdad he was a treasured member of my community who I would visit and pray with every Wednesday. Abu Yousef lived in a very derelict and dangerous part of Baghdad called Jedidah; it was a dark, downtrodden area full of poverty. Every Saturday, the Mothers Union, who were a key part of our active prayer and ministry team, would go and visit old Abu Yousef and take food and supplies to him. While they were there, they would always pray for him and encourage him. At times, other Christians from the community would visit him and sit on the little wall in his back yard just to keep him company.

It was a tough life for old Abu Yousef, living alone in a dilapidated shack. Unacquainted with the luxuries of close family, media, and electricity, he was completely blind, penniless, and trapped in the filthiest, down-trodden part of a city ravaged by violence, domination, and war. Aspects of Abu Yousef's narrative could easily be read as a "New Testament gospel writer's account" of one of the many contemporary blind, deprived beggars in Rome-occupied Jerusalem. One day during one of the darkest periods of the terrible ISIS atrocities, when homes were being plundered and Bibles were being burned to ashes, Abu Yousef's life changed forever.

Due to the shortage of Bibles, many people had never enjoyed the luxury of having a Bible to call their own and had already been forced to share. The ISIS burnings thus turned one tragedy into one that was even more bitter. The level of violation, sacrilege, blasphemy, and spiritual crime that took place on top of the physical torture and violence already surrounding us was too much for me to bear. I will never forget the pain and heartache that I felt as Bibles turned to ashes. My only way to gain spiritual and emotional relief was to fly over to Jerusalem to spend time alone and cry out to God for help. I describe in further detail the sudden divinely orchestrated unfolding of events that followed in my book *The Glory Zone in the War Zone*, but suffice to say here, I returned from Jerusalem to Baghdad completely overwhelmed and overjoyed by God's goodness. God had been faithful. Right there in Jerusalem He provided an intelligent solution; it was a practical, all-inclusive solution that would simultaneously meet the needs of the blind, the illiterate, and the seeing. Abu Yousef's life was about to be beautifully transformed until the day he said farewell to Baghdad and went to his mansion in Heaven.

Many, like Abu Yousef, had regular visions of Jesus in their dreams, but the day I walked into his house and placed the new solar-powered Arabic speaking audio Bible in his hand, he wept with joy. I showed him how easy it was to charge the device by simply placing it in the sun, and I gently led his old, wrinkled fingers to feel the simple on/off button.

The following month when I returned with my usual convoy of bodyguards and army tanks to Baghdad, Jedidah to do my home visits, I went to check on dear old Abu Yousef. When I knocked on his door, there was no answer, so I entered the house and called his name. There was still no answer, so I went through to the yard. There he was, sitting in the sun with his solar-powered Bible talking to him as it self-charged from the ledge on his stone wall. He took my hand and, trembling with emotion, he said these words: "Abouna, for the first time in my whole life, God is speaking to me all day in my house."

Abu Yousef now had a Bible that could speak to him all day; he now had a Friend whose voice he could hear. He suddenly left loneliness behind and felt uplifted by this new source of energy that was awakening his emotions, enlightening his mind, and illuminating his heart with a light unseen by physical eyes. He was blind, yet his inner eyes were being opened anew.

> *Your testimonies are wonderful; therefore my soul observes them. The unfolding of Your words gives light* (Psalm 119:129-130).

On his empty table, this blind man had been given a bright shining lamp, fresh eternal bread, living water, and the richest of wines. Abu Yousef treasured that audio Bible, and a few years later those who entered his home to find that he had passed to glory said the Bible was still talking away next to his cold, lifeless body.

What must we learn from Abu Yousef? We must learn that whether in times of healthy seclusion, western lockdown, loneliness and deprivation, prison lockdown, or wartime isolation, Jesus of Nazareth still desires to turn up on the scene and change everything. He loves each one of us intimately. His affections are forever toward us and His life-giving, illuminating presence can dispel the shadows from any space. He alone is Holy, and He is the Word incarnate.

Be like Abu Yousef and do not reject the exclusive invitation to sit at His banqueting table and dine like a king. Let us not fall into a tragic dismissal of that which is holy. Let us not "tolerate," "neglect," "normalize," or in any way devalue the sacredness of the holy scriptures.

The Bible is not cheap. For some people, to simply possess one has cost them their life. Be like Abu Yousef and treasure the voice of the Almighty; don't just read the Word, listen and absorb through media, soak to it, sing it over yourself, saturate yourself with scriptures. Let them resonate in you and flow through you. Let them soothe you like honey and sweeten the bitter moments of your day:

How sweet are Your words to my taste! Yes, sweeter than honey to my mouth! (Psalm 119:103)

Learn to rest, like Abu Yousef, in the soundwaves of Heaven, and let Him turn your place of restriction into a place of glorious encounter.

10

CAN'T WALK? JUST FLY!

Recently I have found it more difficult to walk due to the effects of MS on my mobility and balance. Through the current reality of becoming increasingly reliant on a wheelchair, I have acquired a whole new awareness of and compassion for those who experience confinement and restriction due to illness or physical disability. While each of us must fervently reach into the Healing God of the Old Testament and the Healing Jesus of the New Testament, holding on to the superior reality that a miracle is just around the corner, it is important to be honest and real about the frustration and disillusion that immobility can cause.

The amount of time that I still spend flying around the globe thanks to an empowering God, a supportive team, and a modern, comfortable electric wheelchair has made me more aware of the fact that I must continue to fly in other ways too. At times, I may feel confined, but when I close my eyes and lift my voice in worship—whether in English, Hebrew, Arabic, Aramaic, or my heavenly language—I fly like an eagle and thrive in the limitless freedom of an open Heaven and an endless sky. I command all my cells to rejoice and I enter into the ease of a new rhythm and flow as the joy of being in His presence energizes my being and takes me to a new place of holy adoration.

Some of you reading this are not confined by disability at all, but you still need to spread your eagle wings and fly. There is a place in the Spirit of limitless liberty, expansiveness, and infinite bliss. Others of you wish that you had the finances to fly to other nations, and you feel locked down and confined by financial lack. Certain of you feel confined by health issues or an array of other commitments relating to your role as a parent or carer for others. Still others of you may fall into none of these categories, but you are scared to step onto a plane. Let me tell you that regardless of the challenges you face, you were born to fly, and you were born to fly high. At times you may fly with other eagles; at times you may enjoy the exhilaration of catching a rare air current that empowers you to soar to new solitary heights. Worship is the greatest mobiliser that exists. Worship is movement because sound is movement. Worship shifts atmospheres, releases joy, and attracts the angels as they join us from Heaven having recognized the sounds of "home."

Despite the frustrations with my walking, I have this past two years literally flown all over the world from New Zealand and Australia as well as back and forth to the Middle East, Canada, America, Europe, and Asia. I have been able to minister life and truth into so many spheres of society—churches of every denomination, parliaments, political forums, embassies, universities. As I fly to the ends of the earth, continuing to speak of the glorious miracles we experience and raise global awareness of the persecuted church, I find a sense of deep liberation. This liberation arises from the fact that I know that I am truly living out the apostolic declaration that "in my weakness He is strong." Throughout this experience, I have come to realize the empowering presence of the Spirit of Might that energizes and fortifies me for each engagement, whether national or international. Similarly, I have learned that just as in weakness He is strength, in confinement He is movement, in disability He is ability, in restriction He is dynamism, in frustration He is reviving joy.

Confined Yet Unconfined

It is interesting traveling in a wheelchair and yet continuing to see the healing ministry as an essential part of my life and calling as a believer. I used to think to myself, "How can I pray for people to be healed when I myself am reduced to walking with a stick and stuck in a wheelchair?"

I will always remember that one recent, glorious night two years ago at Wildfire, Bristol. It was a special Friday night gathering of many passionate worshipers from different church groups who were eager to receive more of the Holy Spirit. After ministering for a short while, I started to receive various words of knowledge. There were certain medical conditions that I felt reluctant to mention as, somehow, I felt unqualified to do so. I heard the Lord say to me very seriously, "Try it and see," so I took courage and released the words regarding some unusual medical conditions. The presence of God was intense in that place, and one of the words I had related to a complex spinal condition.

Many people came to the front and a long prayer line formed in front of me. The first person to whom I spoke was a partly crippled lady with a walking-frame who was responding to the word of knowledge regarding the spinal condition. I was a little tired after several hours of travel and a long session but wanted to minster until God said to stop, so I sat in my wheelchair and prayed for people from there. As I anointed this dear crippled lady's head with oil and released my faith into the atmosphere, she received complete healing.

There it was that from my place of confinement God enabled me to reach into the confinement of another. Around thirty minutes later, as my team and I stood with the leaders waiting to leave, the lady burst into the parking lot, running toward us crying and telling us that this was the first time in fifteen years that she was pain-free. One could sense a holy angelic presence right there in the parking lot, and one of the leaders was covered in silver. Later that night he and his co-leader came to join us a for a late-night coffee and prayer time in our hotel, and his head and face were still sparkling in silver.

As the joy-filled lady began to dance in the parking lot with joy and gratitude, I felt the wave of wonder diminish into a wave of disappointment. In my thoughts, I said to the Lord, "Lord, I am glad that she is healed, but what about me?" Though I had not said these words out loud, one of my colleagues instantly looked over at me and said, "Andrew, that which God has done through you, He will also do to you." This instantly uplifted my faith and reminded me once again of the great faithfulness and miracle-working power of God. With Him all things are possible.

Here is a short report from Matt, one of the leaders who witnessed this great "suddenly" of God:

> I will always remember when Canon Andrew White visited us at Wildfire, Bristol and prayed for a lady who suffered from very serious spinal damage and needed walking aids—he anointed her and proclaimed healing, which followed by her kicking the walker away and later dancing around the car park! I have seen her several times since and she was still dancing and rejoicing that she could hold her grandson.
>
> It was awesome to see the power of Holy Spirit being made perfect through and in spite of such a visible sense of restriction suffered by the very person ministering. I have had the honor of seeing Canon White minister life and healing to so many people, so often from the confinement of a wheelchair. It is so clear that his focus

is on the person in front of him and on enabling them to experience Heaven, despite being in need of physical healing himself. Not only has Canon White spoken so much worth into me personally and made me feel so valued as a friend, but he has inspired me deeply regarding the ministry of Jesus. I think of how Jesus met the needs of the one amongst a crowd. God's kingdom is always about the individual, and I have seen how being restricted does not prevent that.

Watching the perfect ability of Heaven move so powerfully through a person we may consider dis-"abled" has encouraged and inspired me to see beyond my own circumstances and to keep seeking the Father's heart to love people in a greater way and rejoice in their breakthrough, knowing that we all get to share in it.

MATTHEW HOLMAN

FOUNDER OF "HEARYOURWAY"
PROPHETIC MINISTRY AND
WILDFIRE BRISTOL

It is imperative that the Body of Christ in its entirety increases its awareness of those in our communities who are physically confined. Physical confinement can easily lead to a sense of isolation, and, as I mentioned at the start, isolation, pain, and bondage are oppressions not to be celebrated. For me personally, as a well-known speaker and preacher, it is significantly easier than it is for the majority of those enduring confinement through disability and whose very existence, let alone their capacity to minister healing and life, is often devalued or, worse still, completely unrecognized.

It is vital that we, in the community of believers, take very seriously the rights of the despised, rejected, and disabled members of our community. The expression of love, tenderness, and compassion amidst any group of believers can only truly be measured according to their adoration of King Jesus and their treatment of those who are delicate and vulnerable. Only then are we even beginning to advance toward the fulfilment of the two greatest commandments.

Whatever sense of confinement, restriction, loneliness, or weakness you may be dealing with—physical, mental, or emotional—I am here to tell you that you are a treasured, valued possession. You are a diamond in the Father's hand, and He adores you with a passionate, unquenchable love. He esteems and values you as if you were His only child. He is well able to minster His strength in and through your place of fragility and restriction. From your place of weakness and fatigue, He is able to minster fortitude and energy to others. You may feel disabled but with Him you are enabled. Avoid the trap of believing that you can only minister from your place of strength. Yes, it is true that we must optimize our strengths and giftings in areas where we excel; however, I know of several barren couples who, despite the pain of desires unfulfilled, have prayed for other childless couples, which has resulted in miraculous conceptions and births—some of these have even been via social media.

God is not in a wheelchair. God is in *you*! His power is not crippled, and there is no paralysis in Heaven. Never underestimate the limitless power of the Kingdom of Heaven residing inside of you. The great ministry of the Holy Spirit, His authority, and His perfect will are ever self-revealing and ever self-performing. You may still be awaiting your miracle, but turn confinement into unconfinement and give a miracle to your neighbor. Be an instrument in the Father's hands.

11

WHERE THE SPIRIT
OF THE LORD IS...

Even in negative involuntary forms of alone-ness—which may be impositions, inflictions, or punishments rather than the product of a choice to come away, step aside, and self-seclude—we must know that God's presence is still with us.

The Spirit of the Sovereign Lord, which is one of the seven manifestations of the Holy Spirit as referred to by the prophet Isaiah, is the Spirit of

Jubilee, the breaker anointing that breaks chains, releases captives from bondage, liberates, releases, mobilizes, and empowers.

Many who are physically free may be enchained and confined by darkened thoughts, isolated and locked in by negative emotions or traumatic memories, or even spiritually paralyzed due to fear, shame, or unforgiveness. Whatever the sense of entrapment is caused by, there is always a solution. As Isaiah states:

> *The Spirit of the Lord God is upon me, Because the Lord has anointed me To bring good news to the afflicted; He has sent me to bind up the broken-hearted, To proclaim liberty to captives And freedom to prisoners* (Isaiah 61:1).

Likewise, the apostle Paul, who had experienced multiple forms of bondage, isolation, and captivity ranging from shipwreck to incarceration, reminds the Church at Corinth that where the Spirit of the Lord is present, no form of bondage can prevail.

Even in times of brutal persecution, one can experience freedom in one's spirit: *"Now the Lord is the Spirit, and where the Spirit of the Lord is, there is liberty"* (2 Cor. 3:17).

The Nearness of God

Joseph was a man well acquainted with injustice, betrayal, and incarceration. At the instruction of Reuben, he was thrown by his other brothers into a pit which was itself located in a place of remoteness. *"Throw him into this pit that is in the wilderness"* (Gen. 37:22).

Yet like Hagar, who in sadness and despair after being despised, rejected, and displaced from the household in which she served found herself in a remote place of loneliness, Joseph would receive assurance of God's nearness. Hagar's rescue came through the ministry of angels; Joseph's would come through the ministry of God Himself. We know this because the presence of God with Joseph is referred to on several occasions throughout the account.

God saw to it that from being locked in a pit and sold as slave, Joseph was transported to yet another place of confinement, which would in fact be the training ground to prepare him for national rulership. Jealousy and betrayal led him to the pit; false accusation and anger led him to the prison. Yet neither Joseph's envious brothers nor the bitter, vindictive, spiteful wife of Potiphar, incensed by her inability to control and defile this great, pure-hearted leader in training, could prevent the lovingkindness, favor, and protection of God surrounding him.

> *Joseph's master took him and put him into the jail, the place where the king's prisoners were confined; and he was there in the jail. But the Lord was with Joseph and extended kindness to him, and gave him favor in the sight of the chief jailer* (Genesis 39:20-21).

It was Joseph's ability to keep his heart pure and free of anger, self-pity, or retaliation that enabled him to maintain a space in his heart that was tender and open to receive God's friendship and nearness.

He held on to the dreams and visions of his youth and to all that he had learned from his father regarding he nature of God. Joseph's ability to do these things enabled him to maintain great inner strength and resilience. The place of lockdown became the place of unlocking, for it was here that God would use Joseph to unlock hidden dreams that would in turn unlock the great doors of divine destiny upon his life and the lives of others.

The Blood Covenant

As well as being aware of the liberating presence of the Holy Spirit, we must lay hold of the reality of the cross and our eternal covenant relationship with God as sealed by the shed blood of Jesus. The Spirit of the living God and the blood of Jesus are the two greatest chain-breakers. We must invite His presence into every space, and we must affirm our testimony of the victorious, protective, and liberating power of the blood of Jesus.

The prophet Zachariah in his oracle to Judah and Ephraim, when they were at threat of being invaded and taken captive by neighboring nations, reminds the people of their need to hold fast to the blood covenant between God and them. He exhorts them to be filled with divine hope and trust in the strength of the Almighty to protect and restore:

> *As for you also, because of the blood of My covenant with you, I have set your prisoners free from the waterless pit. Return to the stronghold, O prisoners who have the hope; this very day I am declaring that I will restore double to you* (Zachariah 9:11-12).

In the Place of Restriction, God Restricts the Enemy

Daniel was one who really knew how to hold on to his identity as a son of the covenant and fix his gaze on the sovereignty of God. The very purpose of the isolation and confinement imposed on him was to ensure a cruel, brutal, terrorizing, destructive death. The double restriction of the men who were physically tied and thrown into the furnace was one of the worst forms of torture possible. Yet not only was God clearly there in the crisis, but He ensured that there was an absolutely dramatic spectacle of His being there in order to glorify Himself in the face of Nebuchadnezzar. Whatever furnace we may feel ourselves being thrust into, we must hold fast to our identity and ask God to manifest Himself in the midst of troubles. For those experiencing times of great challenge, always remember that there is a fourth man in the fire.

> *Look! I see four men loosed and walking about in the midst of the fire without harm, and the appearance of the fourth is like a son of the gods!* (Daniel 3:25)

Later, in this place of haunting brutality, God reversed restriction and restricted the mouths of the lions. The very tool that the enemy was using to destroy the life of Daniel was the very tool that God was using to preserve life. Closure and restriction of the lion's mouths was sovereignly enforced within the place of enclosure. Creation was forced to align with the will of the Creator.

Then the king gave orders, and Daniel was brought in and cast into the lions' den. The king spoke and said to Daniel, "Your God whom you constantly serve will Himself deliver you." [...] "My God sent His angel and shut the lions' mouths and they have not harmed me, inasmuch as I was found innocent before Him" (Daniel 6:16,22).

Worship Your Way into a New Space

The Bible is full of examples of individuals who stepped out of confinement and restriction into a place of breakthrough. I cannot discuss the power of God to invade and rescue us from isolation and negative confinement without considering the awesome deliverance of Paul and Silas. Like these two apostles, we must allow zealous praise to govern our atmospheres by enthroning Him upon our praises, we must maintain an unwavering faith in His ability to rescue us, and we must trust the perfect precision and timing of His redemptive intervention. He is the God who liberates; liberation is the perfect outflowing of His nature.

When they had struck them with many blows, they threw them into prison, commanding the jailer to guard them securely; and he, having received such a command, threw them into the inner prison and fastened their feet in the stocks.

But about midnight Paul and Silas were praying and singing hymns of praise to God, and the prisoners were listening to them; and suddenly there came a great earthquake, so that the foundations of the prison house were shaken; and immediately all the doors were opened and everyone's chains were unfastened (Acts 16:23-26).

He is the God who divides the sea, breaks up the earth, unlocks chains, causes walls to crumble, breaks down the doors, and sets the captives free. At times His intervention is sudden; at times it may be progressive—either way, we must be like these apostles and refuse to allow the place of isolation to minimize the fervor of our worship or the strength of our faith.

Releasing the Scrolls

It is interesting to me that just as Jesus, the Word incarnate, was born in a dark, unpleasant, undesirable place, so also was much of His written Word. A significant degree of Paul's enlightened instruction to the early church was written in a prison cell. Paul was imprisoned in Rome and was awaiting a judiciary hearing. As a Roman citizen, he had appealed his case to the emperor Nero and was waiting to be heard.

When I consider that there were four key men who were close to Paul who left Rome in the year 62 CE bound for the province of Asia, located in Asia Minor (modern-day Turkey), carrying sacred scrolls that, centuries later, would become four of the most sublime compositions of scripture, I feel amazed.

On bidding farewell to Paul, each man was given an epistle to take to his particular region. As the letters themselves disclose, Epaphroditus from Philippi had been entrusted with the task of delivering the letter to the Philippians, Tychicus from Ephesus had been entrusted with the task of delivering the letter to the Ephesians. Epaphras from Colossae had been entrusted with the task of delivering the letter to the Colossians, and Onesimus (Philemon's slave) from Colossae had been entrusted with the task of delivering the letter to Philemon.

Had the Roman authorities comprehended the significance of these writings penned by an "unknown" prisoner—which presented a composite picture of Christ, His Ecclesia, the Christ-centered life, and the interrelationship of all three—the four men would have undoubtedly been apprehended and the documents seized. Never assume that the movement and release of God's truth in you and around you is subject to your natural surroundings or your emotional state. On the contrary, He will turn the place of restriction into a place of great revelatory flow.

Exiled into Revelation

This great revelatory flow can be seen at its most powerful in the life of John. John's life, prior to being exiled by the Roman authorities during the reign of the Emperor Domitian to the penal colony of Patmos, had been one of un-restriction. From the expansive lake from which he fished and the vast shore regions of Galilee, his daily view was the vastness of nature. Then, having left his trade to follow Jesus the Nazarene, John's life experience became even more expansive as he learned to experience the limitless miracles and infinite freedom of the leader whom he followed. He watched his leader reach into the darkest places of isolation—leper colonies, cemeteries that housed demoniacs, coffins being carried for burial, caves containing the dead, homes containing those dying of fevers—and bring the expansiveness of His liberating presence into every space.

Throughout John's writings, the preeminence, transcendence, and all-sufficient nature of Jesus is emphasized, as is the fact that if the number of miracles performed had been recorded, their quantity would be uncontainable. Likewise, the vastness of God's love for mankind is emphasized both in John's gospel and in his letters.

Aside from the obvious challenges of mistreatment, malnourishment, loneliness, and dread, it must have been a shock to be treated as a criminal and undergo such extreme isolation and punitive confinement. Yet it was on this tiny, thirteen-square-mile mountainous speck in the Aegean Sea that the all-consuming, unconfinable, glorious, transcendent, ascended one—the one with whom John had walked the shores, dined and fished, prayed and talked, the one whose mother he took care of and in whose name he preached—suddenly manifested Himself in full radiance.

> *I, John, your brother and fellow partaker in the tribulation and kingdom and perseverance which are in Jesus, was on the island called Patmos because of the word of God and the testimony of Jesus* (Revelation 1:9).

The light-bearing testimony that was itself the very reason for John's punishment and isolation was a testimony that would be born at a whole new world-changing level from the place of darkness. The light to which John bore witness in his gospel account was the undying light that would reveal itself in dazzling luminosity there in the bleakness of isolation. As with the letters of Paul, the place of punishment became a base for the release of crucially important divine messages to those apostolic leaders who were teaching the multitudes about the divine Messianic identity of Jesus of Nazareth and the promises granted to those who repented and believed in His name.

Jesus did not just come to uplift His exiled friend but to speak to His church. The messages to the seven churches were scrolls directly from Heaven and will continue to be applicable and resound with eternal relevance until Christ Himself returns. Whatever the church type, form, or size, these messages will apply until the end of the age. Around the year 37 CE, a few years after Jesus's ascension, John, accompanied by Mary the mother of Jesus (whom he cared for), had traveled from Jerusalem to Ephesus and was involved in the establishment of the Church base there. The ardent love and devotion of the people reported by Luke in the book of Acts needed to be reignited and rekindled.

After his eventual release from Patmos, John returned to Ephesus with fresh vision and a wake-up call for leaders to revisit their foundations. Across all of the churches, it was vital that compromise, familiarity, immorality, distraction, or tolerance of sin did not overshadow the ardent love for Him who had been their magnificent obsession.

One of my close friends, Pastor Phil Whitehead, is one of several church leaders who has greatly benefited from spending time in stillness and prayer on the island of Patmos. He shares some of his thoughts and reflections:

> We have loved spending time on Patmos over recent years. It is an island covered in hermitage sites where people have come to pray and seek God. Besides the beauty of Patmos, there is a tangible atmosphere of peace where we, as pastors, can come and step aside from the business of church life, slow down, and prayerfully

reflect on what the Father wants to do in us and through us in a fresh way.

John was in Patmos as a compulsory exile in a penal colony, yet it was very much a time of gaining revelation and perspective for him. When he was caught up in the vision that became the book of Revelation, his whole understanding changed. He saw who was really in charge as Jesus revealed Himself as Alpha and Omega—the Beginning and the End. Jesus was far above the Roman authorities that were holding John. Jesus would end all things; He would create a new Heaven and earth with no more pain and death where every tear would be dried away.

Coming from Ephesus were John ministered, he must have been shocked when Jesus declared that they had left their first love! (See Revelation 2:4.) John was called the "apostle of love." His time of exile on this remote island allowed him to see and hear things as Jesus did. Exile was ultimately a time of realignment to Christ's priority and perspective.

PHIL WHITEHEAD

SENIOR PASTOR, KENNET
CHRISTIAN CENTRE, UK

John learned that despite the harshness of the Roman authorities, God had allowed this for His greater purposes. God was in control of Rome, and John was not in fact a "victim." He had been given a high and holy calling. The place of enclosure had been destined all along to be the place of encounter. The remote island that seemed so misaligned and incongruent with God's plans was in fact the place of realignment.

The dramatic unfolding of truth and counsel in the book of Revelation alone is enough to prove that in the most dismal of locations and the most unjust of circumstances, when Heaven's atmosphere floods in everything changes and, like John, we fall to our knees, overwhelmed by the majesty of His presence.

12

JEWELS IMPRISONED

From the moment I first started ministerial training in Cambridge, I developed a deep interest in the care of prisoners. One of my first pastoral studies units was on prison welfare. Initially I studied the theory of crime and punishment, particularly considering the whole issue of probation. I spent time meeting with offenders on probation, observing the probation process, meeting with probation officers and engaging with those who had received a probationary sentence. It was interesting to meet such a wide variety of young men who had committed serious crimes but avoided prison sentences. A probationary sentence basically meant that these individuals were obliged to engage in community service, which was designed to enable them to invest time into the community in which they lived. Community service included a variety of social services ranging from providing practical support in elderly residential homes, clubs, and societies; assisting in environmental projects; and serving in youth initiatives.

One of my desires was to actually live in a prison and experience prison in a young offenders' institute. I was keen to broaden my horizons, enlarge my perspective, view and perceive the world through a new prism, and gain insight into all aspects of prison life, including solitary confinement. Eventually I was selected to go and "serve my sentence" in Hollesley Bay Young Offenders Institute based in Suffolk in the South of England. Several other students on my training course gained similar experience in other prisons.

Hollesley Bay was an institution that basically functioned as a prison. There was a closed unit whereby prisoners were locked in their cells for about twenty-two hours per day. They were released only for prison duties and chores and a short time of physical exercise. I was sent to my section via the chaplaincy unit and was admitted as an authentic "prisoner." Each day I wore the official prison uniform and lived in the bleak, dismal accommodation, surviving on the small quantity of tasteless food served to the inmates. In the section I was in, there were fifty young residents from a very working-class background who were mainly serving sentences for multiple thefts. A few had committed acts of physical violence, but most had been involved in multiple car thefts and burglaries of homes and stores.

Rough Diamonds

It was a very strange experience being thrown into such an intense pool of young uncouth villains who were predominantly from an Afro-Caribbean background. When I was admitted to jail, I was quickly summoned to present myself before a gathering of inmates who had assembled to meet "the new arrival." They could sense I was different because I was well-dressed and well-spoken, and this aroused inevitable curiosity. I was rapidly summoned to an inmate "court appearance" where certain inmates carried out the dutiful responsibility of seeing that I changed out of my normal clothes into my prison clothes. Having people turn up to prison in a smart tweed jacket, freshly ironed cotton shirt, and colorful silk bowtie was something they were definitely not used to. The major question of the day was: Who on earth was I?

These young juvenile delinquents knew I was not like them but could not fathom the mystique and enigma that surrounded me. Their collective conclusion was that I had to be either a pedophile or a secret prison officer. It was obvious that if I was going to experience life as a prisoner, I needed to be honest with them as to who I really was, so eventually I explained that I was training to be a pastor and wanted to learn what I could from them and from their lives. This rather sudden information raised more questions and inspired further serious interrogation: Why would anybody volunteer to be placed in isolation? Moreover, how could anyone even hope to be one of "them" without being subject to the ritual "dorm-run"?

Dorm-runs were the absolute dread of every new inmate. Every newcomer was forced to run down the narrow corridor lined with open-doored prison cells. As they did their run the other prisoners would collectively dive at them, punching, kicking, and viciously attacking with the intent of hurting them as much as possible. When my fellow gang heard that I was training to be a pastor, they had a fearsome decision to make. Would they show mercy? Would they expect me to do the dorm-run? A lot of these west Indian prisoners were from a Pentecostal background and had to fight with their consciences: Could they really beat up a "man of God"?

As these young convicts proceeded to grapple with this great moral and ethical dilemma, I was summoned again and presented with a further question: "Look here man," they said, "we don't want to beat up a man of God, but if you don't have your dorm-run it means you cannot be one of us and we will have to treat you like one of the prison guards." I decided with all certainty that I did not want to be like a prison guard, so I quickly assured them that I would voluntarily go through with the full dorm-run.

I must confess I quite enjoyed doing my dorm-run, and to this day I feel quite satisfied that I successfully accomplished this venture. The normal dorm-run ritual was for the "victim" to retaliate to the attacks of the prisoners and give them as equally hard a beating as they gave you. I proved to be quite good at this as I had a height of six feet, four inches and size sixteen feet and caused them to regret some of their punches. Basically, I was huge compared to the rest of them—still now I have to purchase my shoes in America as they do not make them large enough here in the UK. After the radical exchange of dorm-run beatings, certain of my fellow prisoners whom I still remember to this day—Delroy, Winston, and Derick—decided to call an emergency meeting. They gathered all the other prisoners together and said: "We simply can't beat up a man of God. We beat you up because you said we could do so, but now we want you to give us some of God's power."

As I stood there looking quite astonished, their next question astounded me even more. "Can you speak in tongues?" they asked, with eyes full of curiosity and intrigue as if I were some strange alien from a distant planet. "Yes, I speak in tongues," I replied, to which they responded without hesitation: "Will you pray with all of us now in tongues?"

I returned their question: "Do you pray in tongues?" Immediately, each one of the Afro-Caribbean prisoners, all coming from Pentecostal backgrounds, gave a collective, confident nod. I was unsure whether this "nod" was a confession or a boast. Whatever it was, it instantly aroused indignation and concern amongst the white prisoners who were scared that they were missing out and said they did not know about it. Clearly their egos had been affected as their proud, obnoxious, assertive, macho-bravado, gangster-like stance began to adjust and they looked as if they had been deprived of some deep, sacred, magical secret. The fact is, I was indeed a strange alien from another planet enshrouded in mystique, and they indeed were excluded and deprived.

So it was that, black and white together, we all gathered in the recreation room. We formed a large inclusive circle and I told them to join hands. I then started to pray in my heavenly language, and within minutes I could feel the room fill with tangible, divine love. As we continued to pray, the weighty presence of God descended upon us like a thick blanket of glory. I could feel mercy flood the room and the harsh, sinister, punitive atmosphere shift to an atmosphere of lightness, unity, peace, and hope. Throughout my remaining days in prison, I did my chores, obeyed commands, lived as a prisoner, and responded to daily requests from Winston, Delroy, and Derick to meet and pray in tongues. This was my first experience of Holy Spirit-filled ministry in prison, but it was only the first of many. The best was yet to come.

Unlocking Lockdown

My next prison experience came many years later when I was working and ministering in Baghdad. Danny Fitzsimons had previously been a paratrooper serving in Afghanistan, and, despite not being mentally fit for the job due to severe post-traumatic stress disorder, he had been posted out to Baghdad to work as a security guard for a company that hired staff and placed them in different locations around the world.

I had not crossed paths with Danny during my time in the capital; however, one day I was informed that there was a young British ex-soldier who had been imprisoned for life for the murder of three individuals. This was Danny.

The shootings had taken place during a violent, drunken dispute and a family relative of Danny's contacted me from England. I was also later informed of the situation by Danny's former colleagues who were working in ex-pat security in Iraq. All parties were concerned about Danny's welfare as he was in a weak position being the only English person in an Iraqi prison.

After discussions with senior Iraqi government ministers, I was granted permission to go and visit Danny. Visiting a high-security Iraqi prison was a challenge in itself as many of the convicts there were guilty of involvement in mass murders and executing serious bombings. Visiting Danny Fitzsimons involved traveling with bodyguards to an extremely high security prison based in a large security lockdown area within the remote desert region way outside the center of Baghdad.

Danny was deeply relieved to meet me and had obviously found out a lot about me. We talked a lot about life back home and about the Christian faith. Like many in the military, Danny was deeply patriotic and always talked of his allegiance to the Queen. I will never forget visiting him once on St. George's day when he insisted that he and I stand together to sing the national anthem. As we stood and sang together, the despair in his demeanor seemed to diminish, and I watched those dark, shame-filled eyes lighten with a faint glimmer of pride and conviction.

Over the months, I visited Danny regularly. For several years I visited every Wednesday and was gradually able to impart to him the love and mercy of Jesus. I did the Alpha course with him and led him through the foundations of the faith, highlighting the importance of having a living relationship with Father, Son, and Holy Spirit. It was amazing to observe the radical, dramatic transformation that slowly took place in Danny as he came to a place of deep brokenness and repentance and drew closer and closer to Jesus.

Within the sinister shadows of solitary isolation, King Jesus was wrapping this guilty, wretched killer in garments of light. He was washing Danny's feet and placing a crown on his head. He was moving Danny into the fullness of that dramatic, divine exchange that so many of us take for granted, allowing Danny to stand debt-free in His own holy righteousness. My eyes fill with tears even as I write this. Oh, how glorious is God's mercy, oh how transcendent that divine light which transforms isolation into revelation and turns deathly loneliness into divine dialogue. Readers, this is real—this is Jesus.

I visited Danny as often as I was able to and he became a son to me; he was a person who gave me mutual encouragement. In the darkest hours of lockdown within the war zone, Danny became a symbol of divine liberation and redemption. He was literally in lockdown within lockdown, yet his heart was no longer in lockdown. Danny's heart had been unlocked by the sovereign key of a loving Father.

During the height of the war, visiting Danny became a highlight. Each week, I would make the difficult journey into the desert region to his place of lockdown. We would meet as true spiritual brothers and hug each other. We would always break bread and drink wine as we remembered the great price paid for Danny's and my new eternal identity. I would lead Danny into a place emotional rest as we remembered how it was on the Sabbath day that Jesus ascended into Heaven and placed His shed blood on the Mercy Seat. Danny learned to understand that Jesus was his Sabbath—the resting place for his soul and the only one who could give him rest: *"Come to Me, all who are weary and heavy-laden, and I will give you rest"* (Matt. 11:28).

The food that Danny had in the Iraqi prison was far worse than anything imaginable. In relative terms it would make most prison food taste like an exclusive gourmet meal. The one thing I could do for Danny was to take him a small bar of delicious luxury Abu Afif chocolate from Baghdad's leading chocolate-makers. This I would do every week and it would bring a little sweetness into his world.

Oh, the Power of the Cross

Ephraim the Syrian was a highly significant Syriac Christian deacon and important hymnographer and theologian of the fourth century. Ephraim fought against many forms of heresy and always emphasized the nature of Jesus as fully God and fully man. Ephraim wrote exclusively in Syriac, which is a dialect of Middle Aramaic, and many of his hymns are still sung by Christian Iraqis. One of my favorite lines from Ephraim's writings is this:

He knows that his treasuries abound: The keys of His treasuries He has put into our hands, He has made the Cross our treasurer to open for us the gates of Paradise.[1]

As we reflect on this truth, we recognize the cross itself as that place of torture, restriction, isolation, literal lock-down / "nail-down," and the eternal cosmic key that would reconcile mankind to the Father. I live daily overwhelmed with gratitude toward my Savior, but at certain moments my heart floods with awe concerning the indescribable sacrifice that was made on my behalf. The cross was the redeemer of the secret place. The infinite flow of divine mercy from Him who hung on it was the greatest treasure this world will ever see.

More Prison Stories

There was one other prisoner whom I visited every week during my time in Iraq. This was Tariq Aziz, the former deputy to Saddam Hussein. Tariq

Aziz was promptly put into prison after Iraq's liberation; however, despite regularly trying to share the gospel and pray with him, Tariq never showed any remote interest whatsoever in repentance or in the Christian tradition that he was "traditionally" a part of. There are lessons to be learned from the stark contrast between Danny and Tariq Aziz: God looks at the heart; in fact, all He requires is a tender, repentant, open heart. Is that really too much?

The next major experience of prison life occurred several years later in Nashville, Tennessee. I frequently visited the Riverbend Maximum Security Institution, a high-security death row prison, and there were twenty-four men in the section I visited. Most of them had already developed a genuine, authentic relationship with Jesus; however, they were keen to know more about Israel and Judaism. Thus I was able to help them gain understanding of the Hebrew context of scripture. I brought them all their own prayer shawl from Jerusalem and connected one of the radically converted mass murderers with my good friend Rabbi Melchior, the Chief Rabbi of Norway who lives in Jerusalem.

Despite his busy schedule, he took the time to correspond in writing with this man.

These prisoners took seriously the fact that Jesus was Jewish, and because of the few Christian books they had already read, they knew of the dangers of replacement theology. They had also been taught from the eleventh chapter of Romans, which refers to God's lasting covenant with Israel.

In the sessions I had with these prisoners, I also saw them grow in their revelation of the infinite magnitude of God's mercy and love. In one of the sessions I talked of how God in Hebrew was just known as Ha Shem (the Name). This inspired them deeply as they were all just known by their number, but God knew them as a named individual because God, "the Name," is the one who names and knew each of them by name.

Whenever I visited, we celebrated communion and always had a time of worship. Once again, we would sing together in our heavenly language and rise out of the prison on eagles' wings. I would visit this American prison during the course of many years, and our sacred times together were always filled with grace and love.

As well as spending years heading up hostage negotiations and mediating the release of captives, I have had the honor of meeting with individuals who have experienced the reality of prolonged incarceration—not least with Terry Waite, who was held hostage for five years in Beirut. The first four years of Terry's incarceration were spent in solitary confinement. I also met Nelson Mandela on several occasions, a man who was imprisoned for twenty-seven years. The common feature of these innocent captives was that, in their own words, divine hope became their anchor and their faith in God became their lifeline. I was recently at a joint book launch with Terry Waite in London and there was a profound exchange of love, honor, and emotion. My encounters with heroes such as Terry Waite, Nelson Mandela, and many others have enabled me to gain perspective and reflect about the relative mildness of my own experience of isolation and captivity compared to theirs. Here I refer to the time that I myself was taken hostage and thrown into a dark room—a drama described in detail in *The Glory Zone in the War Zone*.

My time with prisoners and hostages has infused me with a very deep compassion for all those in isolation. As I mentioned at the start of this book, solitude is often a gift to cherish, and even contend for, but we do not celebrate pain and rejection. We do not celebrate extreme isolation, whether for an innocent hostage, a patient in an isolation ward, a lonely person confined to a home, or even an undeserving prisoner. There is a negative form of isolation that demands compassion, sensitivity, and relief-giving solutions, which can only be given fully by the entry of other compassionate human beings, as well as the presence of God, into that space.

Involuntary punitive isolation is not to be confused with the intentional desire to create solitude with God. We must be grateful for judiciary and legislative systems that succeed in removing criminals from society in order to protect its citizens, yet, equally, we must never forget the words of the

King of Glory to the godless, guilt-ridden criminal on the cross. We must always embrace the higher reality that mercy triumphs over judgement and that Mercy is in fact a person.

Throughout all my times ministering in war, siege, lockdown, and crisis, it has been the tangible light-giving presence of the Holy Spirit that has empowered and marked me. Whether lying in hospital isolation units, cornered at gunpoint, trapped in cars, surrounded by explosions, or held hostage by terrorists, I have in all these things experienced the all-surpassing radiance of His glory.

During the darkest moments of the Bethlehem siege (the solution to which I had been sent by the British authorities to mediate) I was rapidly rescued and preserved by angels and later saturated in supernatural gold and silver. In all of these dark, restrictive moments, I have experienced the dramatic intervention of God. Yet I can sincerely affirm that never in my life have I felt the radical, unconditional, overwhelming, all-consuming, unfathomable love of God so intensely as I have in high security prisons and scenes of punitive isolation. Those who are locked behind prison bars are as valuable to Him as we are. They are still the objects of His unquenchable love and we hold the key to their liberation. These criminals and convicts are treasures hidden in darkness.

Note

1. *The Life and Essential Writings of Ephraim the Syrian* (Jasper, Florida: Revelation Insight, 2011), 187.

13

ARISE, ECCLESIA

Divine Romance

The Song of Solomon is one of the greatest poetic books of scripture. It is an intensely romantic poem between two people in deep love. The great rabbis of old saw it as an allegory of the relationship between God and Israel; however, New Covenant theologians have seen it more as a vision of the relationship between Christ and His Church. Over the years, I have been deeply inspired, uplifted, and transformed by the insights that this greatest of Solomon's songs offers us. The intimate relationship between bridegroom and bride and the great call to come away into a place of deep, holy union, rest, adventure, and dialogue lies at the heart of this song.

> *Suddenly, he transported me into his house of wine—he looked upon me with his unrelenting love divine* (Song of Solomon 2:4 TPT).

The Passion Translation of this scripture highlights the fact that our divine lover literally "transports" us from being alone into a new place of romance with Him. He literally moves us from one place to another that we may dine with Him and foretaste of the great marriage supper of the Lamb here and now. The Bridegroom came suddenly and enabled His lover to be transported and "caught up" in the whirlwind of His love.

In both our own contemplations and in our nurturing of lost souls, it is imperative that we highlight the majestic motive of this divine invitation. It is not some collective, cosmic, "impersonal" invite from a distant, mysterious God for any member of "the broken world" to sign up for. It is an exclusively personal invitation for each of us—the redeemed, the prodigal, and the lost—to come and dine with the King.

> Touched with a sensible regret, I confess to Him all my wickedness, I ask His forgiveness, I abandon myself in His hands that He may do what He pleases with me. The King, full of mercy and goodness, very far from chastising me, embraces me with love, makes me eat at His table, serves me with His own hands, gives me the keys of His treasures...and treats me in all respects as His favorite.[1]

In Psalm 23:5, we read of the presence of this great banquet even in times of enmity, conflict, and crisis. In the ancient Hebrew tradition when people of wealth and social standing held a banquet, they would invite only those considered honorable enough to attend. These lavish celebrations were generally held outside, which ensured glorification of the host and the guests who esteemed themselves far more worthy than any inferior passerby or onlooker. These ancient banquets were thus not subtle events; they thrived on vanity and spectacle. If the king held a banquet, his guests were considered objects of the highest level of favor and affection—worthy of only the finest food and wine in the land. To be seen at the king's banquet was to make a public statement regarding one's social worth.

During my darkest times—whether in siege, imprisonment, or lockdown—the reality of the banqueting table was ever-present. My community still testify to the power and depth of this reality as we worshiped and danced together in the middle of the war zone and experienced pleasure and delight in the presence of our enemies.

> *Listen! I hear my lover's voice. I know it's him coming to me—leaping with joy over mountains, skipping in love over the hills that separate us, to come to me* (Song of Solomon 2:8 TPT).

There are many "mountains" and hindrances such as fear, shame, overloaded schedules, grief, or distraction that feel like walls of separation between us and our divine lover. He is indeed an expert at climbing and skipping joyfully up those mountains and pursuing us so that with this joy He may revive, exhilarate, and uplift us.

Ascend to the holy mountains of separation without me.

> *Until the new day fully dawns, run on ahead like the graceful gazelle and skip like the young stag over the mountains of separation* (Song of Solomon 2:17 TPT).

No matter how extreme and desperate our sense of isolation and no matter how far we may feel from Him, our divine lover is literally just on His way to us with His arms open to embrace us and affirm His love for us. Do not look back; look forward, for He is coming toward us with great joy. The more we set time aside to enter this place of divine romance, the more we find our souls warmed and soothed by the all-consuming depths of His love. Whether in our treasured secret place or a place of involuntary confinement, we can experience the reality of being captivated and protected by the fiery, passionate love of our Bridegroom King.

> *This living, consuming flame will seal you as my prisoner of love. My passion is stronger than the chains of death and the grave* (Song of Solomon 8:6 TPT).

Hidden in the Quiver

The place of hiddenness and smallness may be compared to the inside of the leather quiver that warriors either carried or wore to contain and transport their arrows. The prophet Isaiah uses this image to describe his identity as a product of divine creation, a carrier of His call, and a selected possession. The joy of this reality causes us to celebrate rather than resist the place of divine preparation and concealment.

The Lord called Me from the womb; from the body of My mother He named Me. He has made My mouth like a sharp sword, in the shadow of His hand He has concealed Me; and He has also made Me a select arrow, He has hidden Me in His quiver (Isaiah 49:1-2).

Many may be in this place right now. You may feel hidden, trapped, unnoticed, confined in a place of boredom. You may feel static and wasted, tired of waiting to be unleashed and propelled by the hand of God into the dynamic momentum of your purpose and call. If this is your experience, take comfort and confidence from the words of the prophet—you were created in the womb for great purposes, your call is unique, and your journey from the womb to the quiver will soon be followed by a release into fresh movement as you are fired out as an arrow into the exact place God has ordained for you to be. If you remain patient, humble, and submissive to His superior ways, you will not miss the timings of God.

Furthermore, optimize times of quietness to intercede for families and spend time together strengthening the bonds of love. As you do this, the revelation and the reality of Solomon's declaration in Psalm 126 will become increasingly significant.

> *Like arrows in the hand of a warrior, so are the children of one's youth. How blessed is the man whose quiver is full of them; they will not be ashamed when they speak with their enemies in the gate* (Psalm 127:4-5).

The fresh focus on family is one that I have been enjoying these last six years since my return from Baghdad, and I have become even more aware of how blessed I am to have children, both natural and spiritual. Whether we are parents or not, we are all called to be spiritual mothers and fathers to the next generation. We must value the younger generations and highlight to them the importance of maintaining their own intimate dialogues with God and having times of stillness. For these young "arrows," this is the place of polishing, sharpening, and divine preparation for the great and mighty call upon their lives.

Communities of Brotherly Love

One of the essential aspects of my spiritual journey has been my engagement with the monastic community. My grandparents lived near a friary in the East Side of London, and when visiting them I would see the Franciscan monks interacting with people in the neighborhood. These monks were a lot more "evangelical" and engaged with the community than other monks. My first personal experience of a friar was when I was twelve years old and ill in hospital. Several church leaders visited me in the hospital, but the friar was something different. After all, I was a vibrant Pentecostal and I had never met a monk, a friar, or a nun before. I still have vivid memories of the mysterious friar: he wore very long brown robes, and he carried a calm composure and a gentle serenity that no one else, as kind and prayerful as they were, seemed to carry. My childhood mind was intrigued by his appearance

165

and his demeanor, but most of all I was drawn by his "secret" advice.

As I lay in the hospital bed, the friar known as Brother Nicholas taught me to do something that no one else had told me to do. God wanted to speak to me, and rather than just praying and receiving prayers, I should practice listening to God. He spoke to me about being still and fixing my mind on Jesus. He taught me to silence my heart and allow Jesus to bring peace and inner rest. He taught me to listen to the inner voice because God had messages that He wanted me to listen to. He told me that sometimes they may come as faint whispers. I learned the simple key of Isaiah that "in quietness and trust" was salvation and strength.

My experience of the monastic community began in my medical days well before I entered full-time ministry. I regularly went to Alton Abbey, a Benedictine community that regularly welcomed people to come on retreats. I gradually began to long for seclusion and aloneness with God, and this desire became foundational to the life I would eventually lead. I will never forget the inspiration I drew from one of the Northern Irish monks at Alton Abbey. Like the friar, his name was Brother Nicholas and he explained to me the invaluable treasures that one could access through prayer, fasting, and silence in the presence of God. I learned to treasure simplicity and purity, to abide in the "strong tower" of God's name, and to embrace the possibility of an ever-flowing conversation with God.

The seventeenth century French mystic Madame Guyon, who was imprisoned for heresy following her publication of a book on prayer, describes prayer itself as a place of fortification:

> A stronghold into which the Enemy cannot enter. He may attack it, besiege it, make noise about its walls; but while we are faithful and hold our station, he cannot hurt us.[2]

Later, when studying theology at Ridley Hall, Cambridge, I became deeply influenced by a certain nun called Sister Elizabeth Mary who visited the college every semester and spent at least a week with the students. Sister Elizabeth Mary would teach us how to pray and meditate on the Almighty. We had quiet retreats when we stepped aside from studying in order to simply bask in the presence of God. These were times of consecration, inspiration, and oneness with God. We did not call it "soaking," but in essence this is what we were doing—stepping aside from the school to the soaking room. I experienced a great sense of peace, sanctification, and refinement as I allowed my "temple" to be cleansed by the purging waters of His presence.

I was also inspired by the prayer life of a retired professor of history called Margaret Bowker. Professor Bowker told us how, when diagnosed with terminal cancer, she had said to God, "If You heal me, I will dedicate my life to teaching people how to pray." God answered her prayer and she became a spiritual mentor. Professor Bowker taught us to pray the Word of God but also to be very specific in our requests to God so that we could see and tell of the great miracles that would follow. We followed her advice and miracles followed every time.

Later, during my time in the Middle East, I was influenced by the community of the Sisters of Zion, an international monastic community dedicated in its commission to strengthening relations between Jews and Christians. I had been introduced to this community by an Aramaic-speaking German Lutheran minister called Petra who to this day remains a good friend.

I was also influenced by a sister from the Syrian Orthodox community known as Sister Ustina. Sister Ustina was originally from Iraq, and like all Iraqi Christians she spoke Aramaic, a language which years later would become the main language in which I would find myself immersed.

My connection with the monastic community was highly instrumental in terms of what God had planned ahead that I could not yet see. Every encounter was intricately orchestrated by God. I was about to step into a war-zone ministry where I would need to fight hard to find that place of silence, composure, and equilibrium, to remove distraction and fix my gaze on Jesus. I would need to be vigilant and neglect neither the practice of listening to the precision of His voice, nor the necessity to stay spiritually sharp and alert. I would need to step into such a place of divine love and inner peace that I could truly live in fearlessness. I would need to learn from these Middle Eastern communities who prioritized brotherly love, family, openness, and hospitality. I would need to cling to the secret treasures and hidden riches of the secret place and not allow chaos, persecution, devastation, and distraction to rob me of them. The secret place was to be my lifeline.

When I was a student staying in the Maronite convent complex in the Armenian quarter of the old city, I would walk from there to the Syriac Orthodox Monastery of Saint Mark on the northern slope of Mount Zion. The location is believed to the ancient site of the house of Mary the mother of Mark the evangelist, and historians say it is likely to have been the location of the Last Supper as well as the place where the Holy Spirit fell at Pentecost. It was here at the Monastery of Saint Mark that I originally met with Sister Ustina as she was based there. Whenever I visited, we would reconnect, we would talk about her Iraqi heritage, and she would inspire me with her insights and revelations. Almost every day she would tell me of her dreams, visions, and encounters with Jesus. As I listened to Sister Ustina talk, I felt consumed with holy hunger to experience more of the divine supernatural.

One day when I was alone in the solitary chapel of the monastery, I experienced my own personal Pentecost. I stayed for several hours praying, worshiping, and feeling wave after wave of the Holy Spirit flood my body and my soul. Never before had I experienced such power as I did in that place; it was a place where all things suddenly became new—I was experiencing the new of God. At that point in my life, I had no idea of what was to follow.

I realize now that God was allowing me to step out of my own traditions, mindsets, and familiar cultural frames in order to allow these brothers and sisters to equip me for the ministry that was ahead of me. They taught me about the importance of stillness and something of the constancy and permanency of God's loving dialogues with mankind.

Later, I became close friends with the Archbishop of Jerusalem, Bishop Swerios Malki Murad, who was from the Syrian Orthodox community, and once again I was challenged by the depth and simplicity of his walk with God. I also met a wonderful community of priests, a large section of whom resided in Bethlehem—a community with whom I ended up working very closely later in my ministry. This was an extremely humble, selfless, and God-fearing community, highly devoted to prayer and worship, who experienced many miracles and divine supernatural occurrences. Angelic appearances were considered normal to most of this community, and they regularly talked about the dreams, visions, and visitations they had experienced.

In 2002 when working with this community in Bethlehem during the siege, I was asked if I could help provide them with a school. This was one of the most significant early projects that I directed. Once we had managed to negotiate the end of the siege, we found a property that we expanded and developed. The result of this rapid building project was a large school for over six hundred children. Just two years ago, I spoke at the graduation of the first original kindergarten "siege" children who were there right from the start when we established the school. It was overwhelming to see these children, who once had nothing, leave school as well-educated teenagers still ignited, devout, and resolute in their love for Jesus. My team and I were overwhelmed.

As well as simplicity, purity, humility, and passion, what drew me so deeply to the monastic community was their sincere value of other denominations and traditions. The fruits of the Holy Spirit were very evident within their daily interactions, and they seemed to reverence outsiders in a way that many other Christian denominations did not. The honor and esteem they showed for diversity of expression was refreshing and quite different from some of the attitudes I had experienced in my own circles.

The reason I wanted to mention the monastic element to my training is because as a Pentecostal, Jew-loving "glory man," I saw as much passion and love for Jesus in these communities as I experienced in the vibrant, anointed worship gatherings at the wonder-filled Ruth Ward Heflin meetings where I was prophesied over and established in my call. Significantly, it was in the same week of my very first "chapter" of life in Jerusalem that I first encountered both Ruth Ward Heflin and the Middle Eastern monastic community. Ruth had a sincere affection for the monastic community; they were people very dear to her heart. She was a mighty woman of God who relentlessly and authentically embraced the call of Jesus for us to love each other fervently, and in this sense her passion was to see a "Jerusalem without walls."

> Behold, how good and how pleasant it is
> For brothers to dwell together in unity! It is
> like the precious oil upon the head, Coming
> down upon the beard, even Aaron's beard,
> Coming down upon the edge of his robes.
> It is like the dew of Hermon Coming down
> upon the mountains of Zion; For there the
> Lord commanded the blessing—life forever
> (Psalm 133).

This has also become my deepest desire—to experience the precious oil, the deep pleasure, and the abundant blessings that come from harmony, unity, and brotherly love across every denomination and tradition.

All Together Now

The Christian Iraqi children from my displaced congregation, who currently reside in Jordan, still remain on the frontline of executive decisions. One such decision was the agreement to completely discard their denominational labels and to be known simply as "Massihi"—followers of the Messiah. These children are not only products of the great ecumenical oneness that arose from persecution, they are members of a whole new generation of young believers who do not wish to live in the segregations, divisions, and exclusive categorizations of yesterday. They have no incentive to even attempt to comprehend differences in formalities, versions, or rituals and no interest in examining the underlying reasons for rivalry, superficiality, and comparison between church groups. Several of them saw their own classmates beheaded for worshiping King Jesus, and He, for them, is the central point of all existence.

Likewise, I meet increasing numbers of the same younger generation around the wealthy western world who are equally marked by the same desire. They crave authenticity and oneness and they just want to worship their King. Their King is not divided; His palace is not divided nor is His Kingdom—so, quite rightfully, their question is, "So why on earth should we be divided?" This is a generation that craves and requires lucidity, clarity, and deep fatherly and motherly love. We must teach them well and ensure that we are role-modeling and championing Jesus and not ourselves.

We must learn to be throne-centered and to live in worshipful response to Jesus rather than in reaction to the crises that surround us. Those who worship in Spirit and truth release infinite measures of divine light that darkness cannot and will not overcome.

We are called to be one bride with one united voice and one singular, united gaze. Without compromising the call to purity, passion, alertness, sensitivity to the Holy Spirit, and sound biblical doctrine, we must welcome diversity of expression and style and we must choose to celebrate rather than judge cultural, traditional, racial, ethnic, and stylistic differences. There will be new sounds released as ancient sounds of past ages return to the forefront. I even see this in my own life, for I am one whose soaking collection ranges from Misty Edwards and IHOP livestreams right across the spectrum to Hebrew, Aramaic, and Arabic melodies and those great revival hymns sung by the Welsh male voice choir. I am certainly making up for lost time in the war zones of Baghdad when my private soaking collection was limited to just a few tracks on my phone.

If the Ecclesia is to arise, govern, and release the kingship of Jesus in this hour, we must be increasingly intentional in our rejection of division, factions, and small-mindedness. A divided church cannot stand with open arms to reach the lost. I believe this next epoch of church glory will entail a move from de-formation to true reformation. It will see a "re-forming" of the disintegrated bride into a multi-faceted composite *one*. She will start to shine with the intense depth, coherence, simplicity, and purity of a diamond.

Challenges will come, but it is not how we are "pushed down" that matters; it is how we rise. Like David, we must be prudent in speech and our voices must release love, grace, and truth for our attitudes and words are always creating worlds. We are moving into a moment of history when the great resounding plea of our Messiah will start to be responded to in a magnificent way.

> *The glory which You have given Me I have given to them, that they may be **one**, just as We are one; I in them and You in Me, that they may be perfected in **unity**, so that **the world** may know that You sent Me, and loved them, even as You have loved Me* (John 17:22-23).

In order to rise unitedly into the great redemptive Kingdom mandate to prioritize reformation, reconciliation, restoration, righteous governance, and the preparation of lost souls for the return of our King, we must intentionally reject all forms of pride, vanity, compromise, impurity, competition, divisiveness, distraction, and self-promotion. No part of an adorned bride or her bridal dress competes with the other. The idea is itself ridiculous and absurd. The bride is at peace with herself. She is wholly radiant from head to foot. Like her groom, she is *all-together* lovely.

Likewise, we must rise *all together* in tenderness and beauty. Whether in home church, cyber church, prison church, megachurch, boat church, barn church, war-zone church, underground church, or persecuted church, we must choose to ardently value and embrace the treasures and riches of covenantal unity and oneness. We must love and care for each other with fervor and sincerity.

All together we must choose to adorn ourselves in garments of purity, truth, and light. *All together* we must re-embrace stillness, quietness, awe, wonder, anointed worship, sensitivity to the flow of the Holy Spirit, consecration, and all forms of prayer from intercessory to contemplative. *All together* we must passionately re-embrace the call to step aside, reprioritize the "one thing" and love God with all our hearts, minds, and strength. *All together* we must fix our gaze on Jesus so that He may fill all of us with all of Him. *All together* we must prepare for a global harvest of souls.

Arise Ecclesia! All together, we can do it!

Notes

1. Brother Lawrence, *The Practice of the Presence of God* (Renaissance Classics, 2012), 17.

2. Jeanne Marie Bouvier de la Motte Guyon, *Jeanne Guyon: An Autobiography* (New Kensington, PA: Whitaker House, 1997), 26.

ABOUT ANDREW WHITE

Canon Andrew White has served as a peace-maker and mediator engaging with key religious and political leaders in several nations, across differing faiths and denominations. He has a powerful apostolic ministry into the Middle East, particularly Israel and Iraq where he served for 2 decades and led a vibrant congregation of 6,500 people. Canon White's experience of life in sieges and war zones has been marked by signs and wonders and his deep desire is for all believers to know the glorious reality of being "one" in Jesus, our Messiah.

Printed in Great Britain
by Amazon

60062573R00108